Ending Dependency

Ending Dependency

Lessons from Welfare Reform in the USA

Douglas J. Besharov
Peter Germanis
Jay Hein
Donald K. Jonas
Amy L. Sherman

with an introduction by
Alan Deacon

CIVITAS: Institute for the Study of Civil Society
London

First published May 2001

© The Institute for the Study of Civil Society 2001
email: books@civil-society.org.uk

ISBN 1-903 386-12-8

Typeset by CIVITAS
in New Century Schoolbook

Printed in Great Britain by
The Cromwell Press
Trowbridge, Wiltshire

Contents

The Authors

Douglas J. Besharov is the Joseph J. and Violet Jacobs Scholar in Social Welfare Studies at the American Enterprise Institute. He is also a professor at the University of Maryland's School of Public Affairs and director of its Welfare Reform Academy. He is the author or editor of several books, including *Recognizing Child Abuse: A Guide for the Concerned*, 1990; *Enhancing Early Childhood Programs: Burdens and Opportunities*, 1996; and *America's Disconnected Youth*, 1999.

Alan Deacon is Professor of Social Policy and a member of the ESRC Group on Care, Values and the Future of Welfare at the University of Leeds. He has written widely on the debate about welfare reform in Britain and the United States, most recently in *Political Quarterly*, 1998; *Journal of Social Policy*, 1999 and *Policy and Politics*, 2000. His latest book, *Perspectives on Welfare*, will be published by Open University Press in 2002.

Peter Germanis is Assistant Director of the University of Maryland's Welfare Reform Academy. He is author or co-author of numerous publications on welfare reform, including *Evaluating Welfare Reform: A Guide for Scholars and Practitioners*, 1997.

Jay Hein is director of the Welfare Policy Center and research fellow at Hudson Institute. Prior to this he served as a director of Hudson's Madison, Wisconsin field office and manager of a Wisconsin Department of Workforce Development welfare reform policy team. In both of these roles Hein was instrumental in designing and implementing Wisconsin's ground-breaking welfare replacement programme. He is presently co-authoring a book on Wisconsin's effort to replace welfare with a work-based system. He has written for and has been quoted in numerous newspapers and periodicals.

Donald K. Jonas is a research fellow with the Welfare Policy Center (WPC) and director of the WPC's Southeast Field Office. Prior to joining the WPC, Jonas was the Herman Kahn Fellow at the Hudson Institute during the 1997-98 term. He is an adjunct professor of political science at Butler University, where he teaches state and local government. He graduated from the University of North Carolina (BA, 1989), Appalachian State University (MA 1992), and the University of Kentucky (PhD 1998). Dr Jonas is co-author of Hudson's *Health Care 2020*, a book about the future of America's healthcare system, and he is contributing author to Hudson's *Workforce 2020*, a book describing the challenges and opportunities for American corporations and workers in the early twenty-first century.

Amy L. Sherman is Senior Research Fellow at the Hudson Institute and Urban Ministries Advisor at Trinity Presbyterian Church in Charlottesville, VA. Her most recent book is *Restorers of Hope: Reaching the Poor in Your Community with Church-Based Ministries that Work*, Crossway Books, 1997.

Introduction
The Realities of Welfare Reform: Some Home Truths from the USA?

Alan Deacon

During each period of welfare policy change, the alternative to the existing policy seemed impossible, and then once in place inevitable, and when challenged obviously vulnerable. Those who venture predictions with a high degree of specificity about the future of welfare policy should probably be chastened by this cycle
Steven Teles and Timothy Prinz[1]

There are few changes in social policy that have been so radical and so contentious as those made to the US welfare system in the 1990s. There have been even fewer, however, whose early impact has so confounded their critics.

At the heart of the changes was the abolition of 'a right to welfare'. In the US welfare is synonymous with means-tested assistance paid primarily to lone mothers and their children. This assistance is paid in the form of food stamps and cash benefits, and for many years the most important programme of cash assistance was Aid to Families with Dependent Children (AFDC). In 1996, however, AFDC was abolished and replaced with a radically different programme called Temporary Assistance for Needy Families (TANF). The critical difference between the two was that under AFDC benefits were an entitlement. It was left to each state to decide what level of benefits it paid, but all were required by law to pay something to people whose income and resources fell below the limits defined by the federal government. That obligation was lifted by the Personal Responsibility and Work Opportunity Reconciliation Act of 1996 (PRWORA), the relevant part of which declared that it should 'not be interpreted to entitle any

1

individual or family to assistance under any state program'.[2]

States were now debarred from using TANF funds to pay benefits to a family that included an adult who had already claimed welfare for a total of five years during his or her lifetime. They were also to ensure that no one could receive welfare for two years without participating in work activities. Furthermore, a state would incur a financial penalty if it failed to ensure that a stipulated proportion of TANF recipients were engaged in work activities on designated dates.[3] Other provisions sought to influence the reproductive behaviour of poor women, either through direct regulation of the women themselves, or through the payment of financial bonuses to state governments that met aggregate targets. States, for example, were prohibited from paying TANF to mothers under 18 who did not live with an adult or did not attend school, but were to receive an increase in funding if they succeeded in reducing out-of-wedlock births without increasing the number of abortions.

The dual thrust of these provisions reflected the fact that the Act had not one central objective but two. These were, first, to 'end the dependency of needy parents on government benefits by promoting job preparation, work and marriage' (the 'employment goals') and, second, to 'prevent and reduce the incidence of out-of-wedlock pregnancies' and 'encourage the formation and maintenance of two-parent families' (the 'family goals').

The Impact Of Reform

The Act provoked a storm of protest. President Clinton's decision to sign the Republican bill that became PRWORA was famously condemned by one of his former aides, Peter Edelman as 'the worst thing Bill Clinton has done'.[4] Similarly, the doyen of commentators on poverty Daniel P. Moynihan lamented that 'the premise of this legislation is that the behaviour of certain adults can be changed by making the lives of their children as wretched as possible'. The result, he predicted, would be to 'substantially increase poverty and destitution'.[5] Equally forthright was the Nobel

Prize-winning economist Robert Solow. It would be impossible, he argued, for the labour market to absorb a sudden influx of unskilled and inexperienced women workers, and the result would be a sharp rise in unemployment and a drop in wage rates.[6] Perhaps the most significant critic, however, was David Ellwood, who had done more than anyone to legitimise the idea of time limits and who had been the chief architect of Clinton's earlier welfare reform plan. He condemned the 1996 Act as 'appalling'. It offered claimants not 'two years and you work' but two years 'followed by nothing—no welfare, no jobs, no support'. Even worse, the Act would initiate a 'race to the bottom' since those states which did want to promote work-based reform 'may find it too costly if nearby states threaten to dump their poor by simply cutting benefits'.[7]

In the event none of these predictions have been borne out. True, the number of people in receipt of welfare fell by more than half from over 14 million in January 1994 to just under seven million in June 1999. Poverty rates have also fallen, however, albeit much more slowly than the caseloads. The proportion of Americans living in poverty declined from 13.7 per cent in 1996 to 12.7 per cent in 1998. In October 1999 the Centre on Budget and Policy Priorities reported that the proportion of children in poverty was the lowest for 20 years and that the poverty rate for African Americans was at an all time low.[8] Perhaps most striking of all, however, is the fact that between the first quarter of 1996 and the second quarter of 1998 around 740,000 never-married mothers entered the labour force, and the economy generated jobs for them all. Indeed the unemployment rate for this group actually fell from 19 per cent to 15 per cent.[9]

All of this means that the US is currently a great place to be conservative on welfare. It is, therefore, greatly to the credit of the authors of these essays that they resist the temptation to simply rehearse again the discomfiture of their opponents. Instead of simple-minded triumphalism they provide a reasoned assessment of the implementation and impact of the reforms. In particular they highlight three reasons why it is necessary to be cautious in interpreting the effects of the changes. The first, as Besharov and Germanis note, is that the decline in the caseloads owes much to the phenomenal strength of the US economy in the late 1990s. The second, as Besharov and Germanis again note, is that the movement of so many people from welfare to work was greatly facilitated by the expansion of the Earned Income Tax Credit (EITC), which was a key policy of the Clinton administration. Indeed, there are signs that a new consensus is beginning to emerge, with liberals accepting the enforcement of work requirements and conservatives acknowledging the need to 'make work pay'. The third qualification is that the decline in poverty is not commensurate with the fall in welfare rolls or strength of the economy. Jay Hein stresses that many of those who have taken jobs are still poor, whilst others have argued that the families that remain on welfare are living in deeper poverty than ever before.[10]

There is, however, a further and more fundamental point to be made about the effects of the reforms. This is that the success in achieving the 'employment goals' of the Act contrasts sharply with the lack of success (to date) in achieving its 'family goals'. This outcome is all the more significant because the provisions of PRWORA had been shaped by a protracted and important debate amongst US conservatives over the relative importance of these two goals.

Abolition Or Paternalism?

There is a widespread misconception in Britain that leading US conservatives such as Lawrence Mead or Charles Murray hold very similar views on welfare reform. This is as true of those who laud such conservatives as it is of those who demonise them. In reality, however, there could scarcely be a greater contrast than that between the 'new paternalism' of Mead, and the libertarianism of Murray. Although they both focus upon welfare dependency, their analyses and policy prescriptions are grounded in quite different views of human nature, and of the role that public policy can play in changing the behaviour and character of the poor.

Charles Murray has always started from the premise that the poor—like everyone else—are motivated by self interest. He assumes that they will act rationally to better the circumstances of themselves and their families. The difference between the poor and the non-poor, however, is that the former 'play with fewer chips and cannot wait as long for results'. The root cause of the growth of welfare dependency since the 1960s is the failure of policy makers to recognise that the 'behaviours that are "rational" are different at different economic levels'. This failure led the planners of the 1960s to create a welfare system that made it 'profitable for the poor to behave in the short term in ways that were destructive in the long term'. There was no 'need to invoke the spectres of cultural pathology or inferior upbringing' to explain dependency. It was simply a question of the poor making 'rational choices among alternatives', and of people 'responding rationally to the reality of the world around them'. These perverse incentives can not be removed by tinkering with the rules governing entitlement. The only solution is to abolish government welfare programmes and rely instead on the more discriminating provision of charities and local community groups.[11]

For his part Mead dismisses as 'bankrupt' the 'entire tradition of explaining poverty or dependency in terms of incentives or disincentives'. The poor, he insists, will not respond to changes in the framework of financial incentives or sanctions because they are not the competent, functioning individuals that Murray imagines. On the contrary, they are the 'dutiful but defeated' who will not take advantage of opportunities for advancement unless forced to do so. The problem lies in a culture of poverty that condones self-destructive behaviour. The answer to dependency, then, is not for governments to abandon the poor, but for governments to exercise authority over the poor. Rather than abandon public welfare, government should use it to ensure that the poor act in ways conducive to their own betterment and the common good.[12]

This debate between paternalism and abolitionism has been conducted in numerous forums since the mid-1980s.

What gave it a new intensity was the mounting concern amongst conservatives at the rise in the number of births outside marriage, and at the implications of this apparent collapse of the traditional family. In an article in the *Wall St Journal* in October 1993, Murray claimed that 'illegitimacy is the single most important social problem of our time' because 'it drives everything else'. He later told a British audience that communities 'in which a large proportion of the children are born without fathers end up with enormous social problems', and that this is true 'whether or not the mothers are working'. The clear implication was that a welfare reform that 'moved large numbers of women off welfare' but did not reduce illegitimacy would have achieved 'nothing'.

Mead's response to this has not been to argue that non-marital births are unimportant, but that they are beyond the immediate influence of governments. Governments, he says, know 'something about how to enforce work, but almost nothing about how to confine childbearing to marriage'.[13] He has a similarly pragmatic response to other conservatives who argue that enforcing work obligations could be detrimental to the children of lone mothers. Here again the issue is what public policy can actually achieve. Governments know nothing about how to make women better mothers, but it does know how to make them take paid employment. To children, 'functioning parents' are 'worth 25 Head Start programmes' and only parents who work have the self-respect needed to command the respect of their children.[14] The philosophy that underpins this work-first, authoritarian approach is captured perfectly in Hein's vignette of Jason Turner.

The ways in which the Republicans in Congress sought to reconcile these conflicting strands has been brilliantly chronicled in Kent Weaver's *Ending Welfare As We Know It*.[15] In the implementation of PRWORA, however, the dominant impulse has been paternalism and the focus has been almost entirely upon the promotion of work. This is illustrated clearly in Sherman's account of welfare reform in Wisconsin and in Jonas's account of events in Florida.

In stark contrast, a multi-state analysis of the welfare systems created under the Act found that few states had done anything to attain 'the Act's anti-reproductive and marriage goals'. Indeed, the five states that had achieved the largest 'decreases in illegitimacy did not know what they had done to accomplish this, and, in fact, it appeared that at least some of them had done little or nothing at all'.[16] Nor is this surprising. As Rebecca Maynard has recently noted, 'more than a decade of research' has found 'no magic formula' for the prevention of teenage pregnancies'.[17]

Lessons for the UK?

The influence of American ideas and experiences upon British thinking on welfare has been well documented.[18] It follows that there are many similarities between the approach to welfare reform adopted by New Labour in Britain and the former New Democrat administration in the US. Both have sought to rebuild popular support for welfare by enforcing work and combating fraud, both have emphasised the obligations as well as the rights of claimants, and both have given a high priority to 'making work pay'. The most important point of similarity, however, is that in both countries welfare reform has represented, at least in part, a response to conservative arguments about dependency. Both New Labour and the New Democrats sought to draw upon and encompass elements from hitherto conflicting approaches to welfare reform. As Steve Teles has argued, it is this integrative approach that gives some credence to claims that both governments have followed a Third Way on welfare.[19]

These commonalities mean that it is reasonable to talk of policy transfer between the two countries. The obvious lesson to be drawn from the experience of PRWORA is that patterns of partnering and parenting are far more resistant to policy interventions than are labour-market practices and behaviours. As Besharov and Germanis conclude, it will take a generation to find out whether or not the Act has led to a significant improvement in outcomes for children.

Moreover, any attempt to use public policy to discourage non-marital births and promote marriage is likely to face even greater obstacles in the UK. This was dramatically demonstrated by the unprecedented revolt of Labour MPs against the Labour government's decision to implement Conservative plans to abolish One Parent Benefit, an episode that did lasting damage to the credibility of both of the ministers involved—Harriet Harman and Frank Field.[20]

There is, however, a further and even more important difference between the welfare regimes of the UK and the US. This lies in the sharply contrasting assumptions they make about the labour-market participation of the mothers of young children, and especially of lone mothers of such children. As these essays demonstrate, welfare policy in the US rests unequivocally upon the assumption that lone mothers should take paid work, and does not flinch from the implications of requiring them to do so.

In Ann Orloff's phrase, the 1996 Act eliminated 'care-giving as a base for making claims within the US welfare state'. TANF provides for a single mother on the grounds that she is a potential worker, not as someone with recognised responsibilities for the care of children. Lone mothers may be entitled to assistance with childcare if and when they take paid employment, but they can no longer 'maintain a household' without either 'access to a male wage' or themselves 'working for pay'. Orloff goes on to argue that the lack of opposition to this change from 'women's equality organisations' reflects the fact that the great majority of married mothers were already in paid work. 'AFDC rules' she points out 'seemed to make possible staying at home to care for children at public expense—exactly what isn't guaranteed to any other mother or father'.[21] The same point was spelt out by Hillary Clinton in an interview with *Time* magazine in 1996. She was asked whether 'it makes sense to force a single mother of a young child to work'.

> I've thought about that a lot. I think getting up and going to work, going to school and having to make the same difficult decisions about who cares for your children *that every other working mother has to make* is a necessary step toward learning how to be self-

sufficient. Yes, people who are physically able to work ought to work.[22]

There is no such consensus in Britain. Even the very limited measure of compulsion in the New Deal for Lone Parents has been criticised on the grounds that the decision whether or not to combine work and motherhood is a socially and culturally situated moral choice, not a matter of rational economic calculation. At the same time both social conservatives and welfare lobbyists have argued that the imposition of work requirements upon lone mothers would be against the interests of their children.[23]

The critical point is, of course, that US-style welfare reforms cannot be introduced fully in the UK until this debate is resolved. This does not mean, however, that commentators and policy makers do not have much to learn from the impact of PROWORA, and from the essays in this book. What it does mean is that those lessons may not be comfortable ones. Many on the left will have to abandon a knee-jerk suspicion of the American approach and acknowledge what it has achieved. At the same time social conservatives (and some liberals) will have to recognise that those achievements have been possible because, in Theda Skocpol's words, paid work is now 'universally understood as desirable for all adults' in the US, 'men and women, mothers and fathers alike'.[24] This may be unpalatable, and so may be the fact that welfare reform in the US has had little immediate success in achieving its 'family goals'.

Notes

1   Teles, S. and Prinz, T., 'The politics of right retraction: welfare from entitlement to block grant', in Landy, M., Levin, M. and Shapiro, M. (eds.), *The New Politics of Public Policy II: The Persistence of Change*, Washington DC: Georgetown University Press, 2000.

2   Quotations from the Act are taken from Weaver, K., *Ending Welfare As We Know It*, Brookings Institute, Washington DC: Brookings Institute, 2000.

3   In broad terms, the federal government in Washington had
    matched a state's spending on AFDC dollar for dollar. If more
    families were admitted to welfare, then the federal grant rose
    accordingly. This meant that welfare was relatively cheap for
    individual states, and especially for those with the lowest
    incomes per head who received proportionately greater
    funding from the federal government. The 1996 Act replaced
    this matched funding with a block grant, which was based
    upon the amount each state had received in 1993 or 1994. The
    drop in caseloads means that states have enjoyed a windfall
    since 1996. The level of the block grant, however, will be
    renegotiated as part of the reauthorisation of TANF during the
    2000-2002 Congress.

4   Edelman, P., 'The worst thing Bill Clinton has done', *The
    Atlantic Monthly*, March 1997.

5   Quoted in Bryner, G., *Politics and Public Morality*, London:
    Norton, 1998, pp. 173, 198.

6   Solow, R., *Work and Welfare*, New Jersey: Princetown
    University Press, 1998.

7   Ellwood, D., 'Welfare reform as I knew it: when bad things
    happen to good policies', *The American Prospect*, No. 26, 1998,
    pp. 26, 28.

8   CBPP, 'Low unemployment, rising wages fuel poverty decline',
    1999, 'www.cbpp.org/9-30-99pov.htm'.

9   Lerman, R., 'Retreat or reform? New US strategies for dealing
    with poverty', in Dean, H. and Woods, R. (ed.), *Social Policy
    Review*, 11, London: Social Policy Association, 1999, p. 237.

10 Children's Defense Fund, 'Extreme poverty rises by more than
    400,000 in one year', 1999,
    (www.childrendefense.org/release990822.htm).

11 Murray, C., *Losing Ground*, New York: Basic Books, 1984,
    pp. 9, 162.

12 Mead, L., *The New Politics of Poverty*, New York: Basic Books,
    1992, p. 136.

13 Mead L., 'Welfare employment', in Mead, L. (ed.), *The New
    Paternalism*, Washington DC: Brookings Institute, 1997, p. 69.

14 Mead, L., 'From welfare to work', in Deacon, A. (ed.), *From
    Welfare to Work: Lessons from America*, London: IEA Health
    and Welfare Unit, 1997, p. 15.

15 Weaver, *Ending Welfare As We Know It*, 2000.

16 Gentry, P., Johnson, C. and Lawrence, C., 'Moving in many directions: State policies, pregnancy prevention and welfare reform', Paper presented to 21st Research Conference of the Association for Public Policy Analysis and Management, Washington DC, 6 November 1999, p. 15.

17 Maynard, R., 'Paternalism, teenage pregnancy prevention and teenage parent services', in Mead, *The New Paternalism*, 1997, p. 101.

18 Deacon, A., 'Learning from the US? The influence of American ideas upon "New Labour" thinking on welfare reform', *Policy and Politics*, Vol. 28, No. 1, 2000; Walker, R., 'The Americanisation of British welfare: a case study of policy transfer', *Focus*, Vol. 19, No. 3, 1998.

19 Teles, S., 'Can New Labour dance the Clinton?', *The American Prospect*, No. 31, 1997.

20 Walker, 'The Americanisation of British welfare: a case study of policy transfer', p. 37.

21 Orloff, A., 'Ending the entitlement of poor mothers: changing social policies, women's employment and caregiving in the contemporary United States', in Hirschman, N. and Liebert, U. (eds.), *Women and Welfare: Theory and Practice in the US and Europe*, New York: Rutgers University Press, 2000, pp. 142, 152.

22 Sheehy, G., *Hillary's Choice*, (revised edn.) New York: Ballentine Books, 2000, p. 289.

23 Phillips, M., *The Sex Change State*, London: Social Market Foundation, 1997; Phillips, M., 'Workfare for lone mothers: a solution to the wrong problem?', in Deacon (ed.), *From Welfare to Work*, 1997.

24 Skocpol, T., *The Missing Middle*, New York: Norton, 2000, p. 161.

The Florida Devolution Model: Lessons from the WAGES Welfare Reform Experiment

Donald K. Jonas

Introduction

Every so often in American policy making the standard rules of the game are violated and real, radical reform occurs. Political dreamers envision an alternative future, articulate a new way of doing things, and do the tough work of building a coalition of support for fundamental change. Non-incremental policy making—having the courage, for example, to suggest that we could in the span of a few short years during the 1960s build a rocket ship to take humans to the moon—does not come around too often. But these non-incremental changes hold the promise for delivering amazing results. It was not long after the vision of moon-walking was cast that we witnessed astronauts taking giant leaps for mankind and knocking golf balls around on the moon's surface.

But despite occasional departures from the norm, incremental policy-making, the theory that most new policies involve only minor departures from the previous way of doing things, typifies American policy making.[1] American government, divided at the federal level among the executive, legislative and judicial branches and then decentralised to states and localities, is biased towards incrementalism. In our pluralist system of multiple and varied interests clamouring for influence and favours in the political process, incrementalism provides the path of least resistance.[2]

This unique American policy-making DNA usually spawns policy-making gridlock. Years ago pre-eminent political scientist James MacGregor Burns warned of the encroaching 'deadlock and drift' incrementalism produces.[3] But occasionally, as with America's aggressive race to the moon, the traditional American incremental policy-making system is unable to slow down the adoption of a totally new policy approach.

Consider American-style welfare reform during the 1990s. Forward-thinking leaders in states like Wisconsin had for years caught onto the fact that the old way of welfare—providing government cash hand-outs without encouraging individual responsibility by recipients—was fundamentally flawed. And yet despite a variety of policy waivers to the states from the federal government during the 1980s and early 1990s, the basic nature of American welfare policy remained trapped in the straightjacket of incremental reform.

What was needed, and what was delivered in July of 1996, was a non-incremental reform of American welfare policy, a complete break from the old way of doing things. The non-incremental bomb federal legislators dropped that year did away with the old Aid to Families with Dependent Children (AFDC), instituting a new work-based safety net in which the able-bodied would be expected to find jobs. This new legislation, the Personal Responsibility and Work Opportunity Reconciliation Act of 1996 (PRWORA), including the Temporary Assistance for Needy Families (TANF) programme, ushered in the most sweeping social policy changes America had seen in decades, creating an entirely new social contract.

The federal entitlement to welfare was replaced with time-limited assistance in which individuals would be expected to work rather than rely on government giveaways. America's governors persuasively argued to their federal representatives that the problems of the poor were best alleviated at the local level by local officials closest to the issue. Where previously the federal government mandated to the states how they would appropriate and spend their poverty-fighting dollars, under TANF states received a block grant allocation. These block grants came with very few federal strings attached, focusing more on outcome measures (by 2002, for example, each state had to cut their welfare roles by 50 per cent of those receiving assistance in 1994) rather than process management.

President Clinton heralded the promise of this new law in transforming, 'a broken system that traps people in a cycle of dependence to one that emphasises work and independence'.[4] Yet despite Clinton's praise for the potential for reform, many of America's leading opinion formers and politicians foresaw a fraying of the social safety net due to the new welfare reform law's radical changes. The new approach to welfare was 'far more likely to hurt poor Americans than to uplift them', warned the *Philadelphia Inquirer*.[5] The *Washington Post* predicted Clinton's signing of the welfare reform legislation would be remembered as 'the low point of his presidency'.[6]

Senator Daniel Patrick Moynihan, perhaps America's foremost public intellectual whose analysis of the culture of poverty has influenced the course of the welfare debate in America for decades, agreed with these pessimists. Moynihan argued that the best available evidence suggested that the new welfare reform legislation would '... substantially increase poverty and destitution while doing little to change the welfare system to one that provides greater opportunity for families in return for demanding greater responsibility'.[7] Moynihan went on to predict states would suffer near financial calamity, saying that California would lose $17 billion over the next six years and forecasting that other states, including 'Illinois, Texas, Florida—will also bear immense new burdens. I wonder if they are ready for what is coming'.[8]

On many levels, we now know, these states were ready. Florida's reform, in particular, a four-year effort christened Work and Gain Economic Self-Sufficiency (WAGES) at its inception in 1996, has been hailed by federal officials, policy analysts and even former welfare recipients for its path-breaking reforms.

But the Florida WAGES welfare reform effort may have been a victim of its own success, having been discontinued by the state legislature during the summer of 2000. In searching for clues for the next phase of inspired and forward-thinking welfare reform, this essay tells the story of Florida's four-year WAGES programme. What was the basic Florida reform philosophy? How was this philosophy encoded in the WAGES legislation? What were the major WAGES success stories and what are the on-going challenges regarding poverty relief in Florida? What lessons can policy makers learn from the WAGES model to help fight poverty and restore hope to the poor in the future?

The Florida Laboratory

The act of legislatively reforming—or even 'ending'—welfare does not occur in a policy vacuum. Instead, the passage and then implementation of new social policy legislation is directly impacted by a number of larger macroeconomic and sociodemographic trends. Before describing the WAGES programme in particular, it is helpful to first review some of these larger trends impacting the specific research laboratory of Florida.

Florida has been on a seemingly unending demographic and economic boom for decades. Only the twentieth largest state in terms of population half a century ago, during the last 20 years Florida raced past Ohio, Illinois, and Pennsylvania to become the fourth largest American state.[9] Demographers teach us that population growth depends on two key variables: 1) the *natural* increase (the difference between births and deaths), and 2) *migration* (both domestic and international). From 1990-1998, Florida's natural increase accounted for just under one-fifth of the growth in Florida's population. Net migration, on the other hand, accounted for over 80 per cent of the overall growth, with about one-third of the net migration being international and the remaining two-thirds domestic.[10] On an average day in 1998, for example, 1,100 people moved into Florida, while about 550 people left.[11]

As its population has boomed, so has Florida's economy. A state's gross state product (GSP) is a function of the value of all the goods and services it produces. In the most recent year for which we have data (1997), Florida's GSP was nearly $380,607 million, which, if it were a *country*, would rank Florida the sixteenth largest economy in the world.[12] A growing economy has driven a growth in employment opportunities. Florida recorded the highest annual job growth of all American states in 1999, a more than 3.5 per cent change in total jobs over the year before.[13] Florida's unemployment rate sank in 1999 to its lowest mark in 30 years, dipping below four per cent.[14]

It was during these boom times that Florida officials were handed, through the federal TANF legislation, the authority and responsibility for transforming Florida's welfare system. While the economic good times were rolling through Florida's communities, there was still a large, and regrettably stable number of families who were not participating in the unprecedented prosperity. At the point of launching Florida's reform effort, over 150,000 families were still trapped in the old way of welfare, reliant on a federal entitlement that would soon be taken away.

The Florida Philosophy

Anticipating the federal government's revoking of AFDC in favour of an entirely new welfare system, Florida's WAGES legislation passed the Florida legislature a few months before TANF became law. WAGES instituted an entirely new public policy approach to improving the lives of the poor. As the accompanying text box reveals, rather than a minor tweaking of eligibility rules or the implementation of a handful of pilot projects, WAGES instituted a fundamental reworking of the social contract for the poor. It

Important components of the WAGES welfare reform legislation:

- Placing a 48-month lifetime limit on benefits;
- Requiring adults to work or engage in work activities;
- Establishing immediate sanctions for people who do not comply with work requirements;
- Providing transitional childcare for participants;
- Requiring teen parents to live at home under adult supervision and stay in school.

instituted strict time limits for benefits, and established a rigorous work-based safety net with real penalties for non-compliance.

The Florida philosophy for welfare reform was rooted in three key principles:

1. A 'work-first' programme design with 'tough-love' time limits on lifetime assistance;

2. Local control of programme dollars coupled with local accountability for results;

3. A strategic reaching-out to non-governmental partners in the search for a better way to address the needs of the poor.

Work first with time-limits

American policy-makers and the general public in the 1990s became increasingly aware of the hazardous consequences of long-term receipt of government cash assistance. Individuals receiving welfare support were required neither to engage in productive work nor to upgrade individual skills in return for public assistance. Under the old system, individuals meeting certain eligibility guidelines were entitled to government cash, and, not surprisingly, many found themselves trapped in a cycle of welfare dependency.

Shielded from the labour market by well-intentioned public policies, individuals tethered to the welfare state were missing out on the opportunity to share in the spoils of America's economic prosperity. In recent decades, both well-to-do and low-income Americans have seen their incomes rise over time. Consider data from the longest panel survey ever done on Americans' earnings, covering a nearly three- decade period from the mid-1970s to the early 1990s (Table 1, p. 18).

We see in this long-term evaluation of individual Americans' income earnings that of those in the lowest quintile in 1975, almost all (nearly 95 per cent) moved up the income mobility ladder during the next 25 years. Further, W. Michael Cox and Richard Alm report that those in the bottom 20 per cent in 1975 experienced an inflation-adjusted gain of $27,745 in average income by 1991 (while for those who began in the top fifth in 1975, the increase was only $4,354). The rich were getting a bit richer, but the poor, especially those who entered the labour market and stayed in productive employment, experienced an even greater percentage boost in income.[15]

Table 1
Upward Mobility

Income Quintile, 1975	% in each Quintile, 1991				
	1st	2nd	3rd	4th	5th
1st (lowest)	5.1	14.6	21.0	30.3	29.0
2nd	14.6	21.0	20.3	25.2	26.8
3rd (middle)	3.3	19.3	28.3	30.1	19.0
4th	1.9	9.3	18.8	32.6	37.4
5th (highest)	0.9	2.8	10.2	23.6	62.5

Source: University of Michigan Panel Survey on Income Dynamics, as reported in Cox, W.M. and Alm, R., *Myths of Rich and Poor*, 1999.

The challenge for welfare reformers would be to first move job-ready individuals off public assistance and into productive employment, and eventually towards individual self-sufficiency. During the early 1990s Florida officials experimented with a variety of pilot projects designed to redirect Florida's welfare programme towards a system that encouraged long-term attachment to productive work. One particular project, the Family Transition Program (FTP), limited federal AFDC benefits to two years for most participants (and to three years for those with special needs). This programme, with its particular emphasis on strict time limits for receipt of government cash support, garnered close attention from state policy-makers.[16]

Former Democratic Governor Lawton Chiles took particular notice of FTP, authorising the expansion of this pilot project—including its emphasis on time-limited benefits—from a small mandatory effort in one Florida county (Escambia) to six additional sites across the state (Duval, Lee, Orange, Pinellas, St. Lucie and Volusia counties) in 1995. Through experimental programmes like FTP, Florida officials acquired home-grown data to support using time-limited benefits to hasten the exit of individuals from public welfare dependency.

In the WAGES legislation, Florida legislators elected to institute limits even more stringent than the federal guidelines, placing a 48-month lifetime limit on benefits. With these strict time limits in place, the average length of stay on welfare in Florida plunged from nearly two years at the inception of WAGES in 1996 to just under eight months by July of 1999.[17] Less than one per cent of the over 150,000 families on welfare when the programme began faced time limits on cash assistance three years into the programme.[18]

Local control and local accountability for local results

A critical piece of the reform philosophy differentiating Florida from many other American states is an emphasis on local control coupled with local accountability for performance and results. Florida Senate President Toni Jennings, a key architect in the early crafting of the WAGES legislation, in reviewing some of the early successes of WAGES at a recent statewide conference, noted that: 'What works in the Panhandle is not necessarily good for Miami. We needed each of you to go forth and do what is right for your community, not what Tallahassee thinks is right for all communities.'[19]

In the new WAGES legislation, 24 regional boards were given responsibility for identifying community resources to meet programme goals. (In 20 of the 24 regions, welfare boards joined forces with existing workforce boards.) These regional boards could develop their own funding strategies, and were given the authority to plan, coordinate, and direct the delivery of welfare services within their local region.[20]

At the state level, a 17-member State WAGES Board (comprised of volunteers with private sector experience and high-ranking members of various state departments and agencies) provided oversight to the 24 regional operations. Michael Poole, Chairman of the WAGES Board, described the primary function of his State Board as being that of a '...holding company that oversees 24 subsidiaries' who were given the money and accountability to move individuals from the welfare rolls to employment.[21] Florida's WAGES programme designers believed local regions had a much better understanding of the strengths and weaknesses of their community than any politician or bureaucrat located miles away.

The WAGES administrative office would set up shop in Tampa, the booming coastal city on Florida's central Gulf Coast. Thus, a devolution of policy-making responsibility away from Tallahassee was coupled with the physical removal of administration of the state programme from the Capitol in Tallahassee. To manage the newly created office, former Governor Chiles looked to local Tampa leadership to drive the programme, and found in Phyllis Busansky an ideal candidate to launch this new programme. Ms Busansky, a former Hillsborough County Commissioner, had gained national notoriety for her tireless efforts in assisting the medically indigent in her community. She had recently been named by *Governing Magazine* its public official of the year, and her leadership skills and commitment to improve the lives of Florida's less fortunate citizens gave the WAGES programme a high public profile.[22]

To promote work over welfare, the WAGES legislation encouraged local officials to focus on 'results rather than process'.[23] Instead of micro-managing the policy process and reform agenda in each of the local regions, State WAGES Board members served as overall programme monitors. A set of results-oriented monthly cash assistance caseload information—including total cash assistance expenditures and the number of families across the state and within each region receiving assistance—became perhaps the most critical set of evaluation data for the State Board.

Throughout the life cycle of the WAGES programme, nearly every coalition met or exceeded nearly every programme goal. And the regions, by and large, were not simply hustling individuals into dead-end jobs. President Clinton's Department of Health and Human Services, acknowledging the remarkable success of Florida's decentralised effort, awarded Florida a nearly $7 million bonus for recording the best job retention and earnings rates for former welfare clients in the country.[24]

While the vast majority of the regions performed above expectations, there was one glaring outlier: Miami-Dade/Monroe County. A few years into WAGES the Miami area reform effort was in cardiac arrest. The largest metropolitan area in Florida and home to the largest percentage caseload in the state, Miami was failing on a number of fronts. The overall caseload numbers for Miami, while shrinking, were not keeping pace with the remarkable reductions occurring across the state. Thousands of individuals potentially eligible for WAGES services were simply unaccounted for.[25] Disjointed local service delivery systems and divided administrative entities were not communicating effectively to improve the situation.

Empowered by Florida statutes to rectify the situation,[26] the State WAGES Board placed Miami on 'administrative watch', advising local officials to either quickly fix the situation or face losing their charter to deliver services.[27] The State Board directed Miami officials to create a Corrective Action Management Team (including workforce development experts from within Miami and across the state) to evaluate the existing service delivery system and develop a consolidated strategy to reverse Miami's troubled programme. Their extensive reform programme proved fruitful. Surrogates from the Miami-Dade Mayor's office took personal responsibility for revitalising the programme. One of the first, critical steps of this local effort was simply getting a handle on the population at hand. Nearly 10,000 clients who had previously been dumped into the data tracking black hole of 'No Recorded Activity' were contacted and brought back into the WAGES information tracking system. The Corrective Action Management Team also mandated more systematic reforms to the local effort, including the introduction of an overall programme monitoring capacity and the development of an ideal service delivery system to replace the previous broken model.[28]

Reaching out beyond the public sector walls

In addition to installing strict time limits for benefits and giving real power and accountability to local communities for performance results, another hallmark of the Florida welfare reform philosophy was a conscious reaching out beyond traditional public sector approaches for help. Consider Florida's efforts to include private sector citizens, those with market-tested business skills and real-world business experience. By state law, voluntary private sector citizens had to occupy half the seats on the State WAGES Board and half the seats on each of the local boards. With an extremely tight labour market in Florida during the late 1990s, the private sector employer community had a particular interest in successful welfare reform: they needed workers. Finding and then holding onto qualified workers was a top concern of employers across the state.[29] Unfortunately, businesses seemed reluctant to consider former welfare recipients as employees. In surveys, three out of four business sector respondents said they had not hired someone on welfare in the last few years.[30] But of those who did hire welfare recipients, more than 80 per cent said they were satisfied and would hire welfare recipients again in the future.[31]

To improve the employability of former welfare recipients and to expose the broader employer community to this new source of labour that would be leaving the welfare rolls, the State WAGES Board requested help from a Florida pro-business group. The Orlando Regional Chamber of Commerce stepped forward with a break-the-mould private sector model for welfare system reform.

The traditional welfare-to-work model—in which resources and operational energies target primarily the job seeker—was discarded. In the Chamber's reformulated model, the needs of employers—including an assessment of the kinds of skills and abilities employers were looking for in the labour force—took top priority.

Initial Chamber research uncovered widespread support for business leadership in the welfare reform effort. (For example, nearly nine of ten respondents in an early Chamber survey agreed that 'business should provide leadership in helping move people from welfare to work'.)[32] Workforce 2020 staff would become advocates for businesses, finding out what employers desired from the local system and then leading the charge in promoting service delivery reforms that addressed the needs of employers. Day-long Academies of Learning (which attracted over 1,000 employer representatives in just over a year) would expose local business leaders to best practices in the hiring and retention of low-income workers. Follow-up Business Roundtables devoted to specific industries or topics of interest would produce practical, employer-driven suggestions on how to redirect the local public workforce development system towards satisfying employer needs.

Figure 1
WorkForce 2020 Welfare-to-Work Model

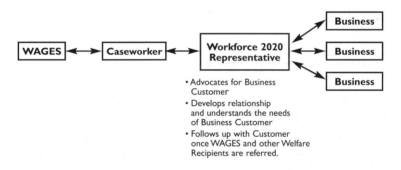

Source: Orlando Regional Chamber of Commerce

The community of faith also played an important role in the Workforce 2020 model for reform. The Jobs Partnership (TJP), a North Carolina Christian-centred organisation, was recruited by Chamber officials to help develop a Central Florida model of their successful programme. Currently active in eight states with more than 100 churches, TJP incorporates a faith-based study curriculum with business-oriented skill development classes for the poor and others in need of help. Mentors from local churches commit to personally working with participants for a minimum of 24 months, staying with individuals as they confront the many challenges involved in transitioning from welfare to self-sufficiency. Between 1996 and 1999, over 90 per cent of Jobs Partnership participants in the flagship Raleigh, North Carolina programme maintained steady employment. Similar success rates for participants in TJP programmes across the country are not uncommon. The key to the success of The Jobs Partnership, says Chris Mangum, co-founder of TJP, is the union between the community of faith and the business community to uplift the lives of the less fortunate. 'In our society, people tend to isolate themselves when other people are hurting but what we need most is the gift of you and me—of ourselves affirming the value and dignity of our neighbours,' Mangum says. 'When you scrape away the blisters of joblessness, you often find areas of distress that exceed the help that is easily available', Mangum continues. 'But unless you deal with the origins of the problem, then all the scraping might be wasted.'[33]

WAGES Makes An Impact

The WAGES model for reform—based on a 'work-first' programme with 'tough-love' time limits on lifetime assistance, local control and accountability for results, and strategic partnerships beyond the public sector—proved successful. Of the eight largest American states, Florida registered the greatest cash-assistance caseload reduction, an 81 per cent drop in the number of families on welfare and subject to time limits from the beginning of the programme in 1996 to the end of WAGES four years later.[34]

Of course, there was more to this welfare reform story than simply enlightened public policy. Undoubtedly, Florida's welfare reformers embarked on their efforts under fortuitous economic conditions. Heading off to this new model for welfare during the longest economic expansion in American history made available new work opportunities for workers of all skills and at different stations in life. And the state of Florida itself—its inviting climate, quality of life, and diverse mix of urban and rural areas—also made the job of luring workers into the labour market much easier.

Figure 2
Total Number of Cash-Assistance Families

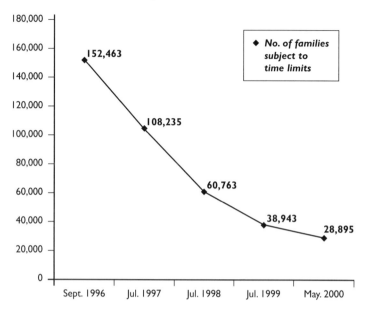

Source: Florida Department of Children and Families

But surveys revealed that most former welfare recipients appreciated the public policy push away from dependency. In a March 1999 report for the WAGES Board about the living circumstances of people who had at some point received WAGES cash benefits but had subsequently left the WAGES programme, a majority of respondents expressed satisfaction with the programme (Table 2 p. 26). Over half said they were either much better off or a little better off. Almost 70 per cent said they would not go back to the old welfare system even if they could.

While most former cash recipients expressed satisfaction with the programme, not all was wine and roses. In rewiring the nature of public assistance, not every individual would be expected to seamlessly ease from government dependency to self-sufficiency. Nearly 20 per cent of respondents in the same study said their conditions were now either a little worse or much worse. Three-fifths said they were now falling behind in paying their utility bill.[35]

Table 2
Since Leaving WAGES, How Are You?

	%
Much better off	26.1
A little better off	24.7
About the same	24.3
A little worse	10.3
Much worse	6.9
Don't know	4.6
Refused to answer	2.4

Note: N = 1,007
Source: Crew Jr., R.E. and Eyerman, J., 'After WAGES: Results of the Florida Study', Florida State University, March 1999.

Of course, while entitlement to welfare cash assistance was over, other basic support systems remained intact, including Medicaid (healthcare coverage for the poor and elderly), school lunch, fuel assistance, rent subsidy and food stamps. In the rush to reform welfare, officials at the local level may have neglected vigilantly to articulate to participants that these other public safety net programmes were still available. For example, in the previously mentioned March 1999 report for the WAGES State Board, nearly half of respondents did not know they were still eligible for food stamps, and over half did not know they could get public childcare assistance.[36] An autumn 1999 report from the Florida Inter-University Welfare Reform Collaborative (a collection of social policy researchers from major Florida universities) noted that the primary challenge for WAGES three years into the reform effort was policy implementation.[37] Case workers, for example, were still not being adequately trained in policies and procedures relating to WAGES.

There were other implementation and operational mistakes with WAGES. Miami, as previously noted, suffered a number of early implementation setbacks before eventually straightening course. Some of the State WAGES Board's pilot projects, including an employment project designed to create jobs for former welfare recipients in economically depressed areas, fell far short of programme goals for a variety of reasons, including the absence of a clearly defined mission and purpose.[38] And many private sector board members, those individuals sitting on over half of the welfare board seats across the state, felt unprepared for the enormity of their new responsibilities. In surveys these private sector citizens expressed strong interest in receiving more training on how to be more effective in their role as community leaders.[39]

Neo-genesis Of Florida Welfare Reform: Preparing For The Future

Despite a number of implementation hiccups, in terms of meeting its overarching legislative mandate of moving individuals away from dependency on government cash support and towards self-sufficiency, WAGES worked. The model was so successful, in fact, it met the happy fate of precious few other public sector programmes: WAGES was discontinued during the summer of 2000. Workforce Florida Inc (WFI), a brand new public-private partnership designed to funnel nearly every federal and state welfare and workforce funding dollar through a single statewide entity, began operations in July of 2000.[40]

The closing down of WAGES and beginning of WFI heralds the end of the initial wave of late-1990s American-style welfare reform and the beginning of a new era. Biologists call early human life cell formation a neo-genesis, or a 'new birth' of tissue formation. American welfare reform is undergoing its own 'new birth'. The challenge now is two-fold: 1) keep those who are working gainfully employed and on the upward mobility path and 2) devise new strategies for the long-term hard-to-serve and other neighbours in need who for many reasons are not moving towards self-sufficiency.

Reformers know that keeping individuals attached to consistent employment increases the likelihood of avoiding a relapse to welfare dependency. In Florida, about one out of three individuals on the total welfare caseload (in 1999) were return customers who had only been away from the welfare system for less than two months. These folks were shuffling back-and-forth through the government cash turnstile, unable to anchor themselves to a steady job. On the other hand, those individuals who locked onto steady employment in the labour force were much less likely to come back to welfare for assistance. If individuals could keep a job for at least six months, the likelihood of returning to welfare dropped substantially. (Only seven per cent of the return cases in 1999 represented those who had kept steady employment for at least six months.)[41]

Public sector planners in Florida and other states, flush with government surpluses, have a seemingly unending artillery of economic support programmes and other economic incentive proposals at their disposal. Many of these worthy programmes promise to go a long way towards meeting the needs of those currently in the workforce and other job-ready individuals seeking just a little extra help to move towards self-sufficiency. The new Workforce Florida initiative does in fact bring together a host of public sector poverty fighting programmes designed to keep Floridians at all income levels in the workforce. These programmes include an array of new and expanded programmes including, for example, increased childcare and transportation eligibility cut-off levels and special programmes for workers of all ages to get training to pass high school equivalency exams.[42]

But a key lesson from the WAGES experiment teaches that there is much more to welfare reform than just fine-tuning economic support programmes. Private sector citizens must become more intimately engaged in welfare reform. Fundamental system reform requires paying close attention to not only the supply end of the equation—those folks leaving welfare—but also to the employers on the demand side.

Florida welfare reform officials recognised this need to engage employers in the search for solutions. Over half of all the positions on Florida's WAGES' boards were filled by private sector citizens. In the new Workforce Florida, Inc. model, private sector representatives continue their strong presence on boards, again occupying half of all the local workforce board positions. In Orlando, Workforce 2020 became an advocate for the employer community, advancing ways to recruit, train, and retain a competitive workforce. The focus was not only on raising awareness in the business community of the many issues surrounding welfare reform, but also on utilising the knowledge and expertise of private sector business leaders to improve the fundamental operation of the local welfare delivery system. At the end of its first year of operation, Workforce 2020's successful reform model generated welcome replication efforts in six additional communities across Florida, sparking wide interest in the private sector in the power of business-driven reform.

Policy makers found great success during the first wave of welfare reform in transitioning job-ready participants into the labour force. Today, many of those who have not progressed towards steady employment have needs perhaps better addressed by groups outside the public sector, including religiously-inspired groups and other non-governmental organisations. With a goal of serving as the 'civic switchboard' connecting federal and state funding with local private and not-for-profit agencies, including faith-based organisations, Governor Jeb Bush's Office of Urban Opportunity will establish 20 Front Porch Florida (FPF) communities by 2002. FPF pulls in a range of community poverty-fighting partners, empowering urban residents to define and develop solutions to their local problems.[43]

And we now have compelling data on the long-term negative impact of absent fathers on the lives of our children. Without a father around, kids are five times more likely to live in poverty, twice as likely to commit a crime, over twice as likely to abuse alcohol or drugs and twice as likely to drop out of school.[44] Too many fathers are not playing a meaningful role in the lives of their children. It is estimated that nearly one in three of Florida's kids do not have their father living in their home with them.[45] Former Indianapolis Mayor Stephen Goldsmith notes that there are a whole range of issues involved in the new movement to promote responsible fatherhood, including '...connecting dad to work; connecting the dad to the child; connecting the dad's money to the child; and connecting the dad personally and socially to the child'.[46]

Florida officials heeded this call to encourage responsible fatherhood, providing incubation grants to promote a variety of grassroots initiatives across the state. For example, Reading Family Ties works with correctional institutes in a number of counties, providing inmates the opportunity to read or tell a story to their children. A Dade County fatherhood training programme targets teenage males, helping them understand the principles of fatherhood, including the importance of nurturing the children they may eventually father. Other programmes, such as the Partners in Fatherhood in Escambia County, identifies fathers before and at the birth of their child, providing these dads with the training and support they need to be a responsible father.[47]

Conclusion

The WAGES philosophy for reform left many lessons in its wake. Given the right economic circumstances and policy incentives, the vast majority of welfare dependent individuals can make a successful transition to gainful employment. Localities can be trusted to deal aggressively and appropriately with the needs of the less fortunate in their neighbourhoods. With proper oversight, even those communities that stumble in their initial reform efforts can be redirected.

Of course, many of the root causes of poverty did not magically disappear during the WAGES experiment. Too many communities face a depressing poverty of spirit and an absence of hope. In the future, public policies designed to strike at the heart of poverty, including fatherhood initiatives aimed at promoting responsible parenting, will lead the way. And new initiatives aimed at uplifting neighbourhoods through strategic partnerships with non-governmental actors, including mission-based, religiously-inspired organisations, will be in the vanguard of tomorrow's welfare reform efforts.

As a non-incremental policy change, WAGES proved a successful model for breaking away from the old way of welfare. Today, Floridians seeking to escape poverty interact with an entirely new workforce development system, one that sees the needs of the poor as part of a broad continuum of workforce development services for the people of Florida. Of course, as with any fundamental policy change, not all aspects of the Florida reform programme went smoothly, and there still remain those who have not achieved true self-sufficiency. These individuals require new policy ideas. To Florida officials' credit, a lasting legacy of the WAGES model is a willingness to think creatively and to experiment with using non-traditional partners and approaches in the effort to improve the lives of the poor.

Notes

1 See, for example, Beam, D.R. and Conlan, T.J., 'Solving the riddle of tax reform: party competition and the politics of ideas', *Political Science Quarterly*, Summer 1990, Vol. 105, Issue 2.

2 Beam and Conlan, 'Solving the riddle of tax reform: party competition and the politics of ideas',1990.

3 MacGregor Burns, J., *The Deadlock of Democracy*, Englewood Cliffs, NJ: Prentice Hall, 1963. As quoted in Beam and Conlan, 'Solving the riddle of tax reform: party competition and the politics of ideas', 1990.

4 White House Office of the Press Secretary, Statement by President Bill Clinton on July 31, 1996. Available on the internet at: (http://www.libertynet.org/edcivic/welfclin2.html).

5 'Reform on the cheap', *Philadelphia Inquirer*, 22 July 1996.

6 'A children's veto', the *Washington Post*, 25 July 1996.

7 From Senator Moynihan's US Senate speech on 1 August 1996.

8 From Senator Moynihan's US Senate speech on 1 August 1996.

9 'Florida Demographic Summary', Office of Economic and Demographic Research for the Florida Legislature: (http://www.state.fl.us/edr/population/popsummary.htm).

10 'Florida Demographic Summary', Office of Economic and Demographic Research for the Florida Legislature: (http://www.state.fl.us/edr/population/popsummary.htm).

11 'Florida 1998-1999', Office of Economic and Demographic Research for the Florida Legislature. For further detail see also the US Bureau of Labor Statistics: (http://www.bls.gov/cpshome.htm) and the US Department of Commerce, Bureau of Economic Analysis: (http://www.bea.doc.gov/bea/regional/data.htm).

12 'Florida 1998-1999', Office of Economic and Demographic Research for the Florida Legislature. For further detail see also the US Bureau of Labor Statistics: (http://www.bls.gov/cpshome.htm) and the US Department of Commerce, Bureau of Economic Analysis: (http://www.bea.doc.gov/bea/regional/data.htm).

13 US Department of Labor, Bureau of Labor Statistics: (http://www.bls.gov/cpshome.htm) and Florida Department of Labor and Employment Security, Office of Labor Market Statistics.

14 US Department of Labor, Bureau of Labor Statistics: (http://www.bls.gov/cpshome.htm) and Florida Department of Labor and Employment Security, Office of Labor Market Statistics. Actual 1999 unemployment was 3.86 per cent.

15 Cox, W.M. and Alm, R., *Myths of Rich and Poor: Why We're Better Than We Think*, New York: Basic Books, 1999.

16 'Governor Chiles Establishes Florida as National Welfare Reform Leader: Signs WAGES Legislation', Florida Governor's Office, 16 May 1996.

17 Florida Department of Children and Families, as reported on the WAGES web site at: 'http://www.wages.org/wages/fastfacts/fastfacts_avgstay.htm'.

18 Florida Department of Children and Families, as reported on the WAGES web site at: (http://www.wages.org/wages/fastfacts/fastfacts_reachinglimits.htm).

19 January 2000 *WAGES Works Newsletter*. The official newsletter of Florida's Welfare Reform Program.

20 F.S. 414.028(4).

21 Testimony of Michael Poole, Chairman, Board of Directors, State of Florida Work and Gain Economic Self-Sufficiency (WAGES) Program to the United States House of Representatives Committee on Government Reform, 22 April 1998.

22 For a list of *Governing Magazine* winners, see: (http://www.governing.com/poy/poyold.htm).

23 F.S. 414.025(3).

24 *WAGES Works Newsletter*, January 2000.

25 State WAGES Board Agenda Item: Update on Miami-Dade Coalition, 14 June 2000.

26 F.S. 414.028(9).

27 Yanez, L., 'Dade district ordered to show history of hiring; Welfare-to-Work employees lack proper education', *Sun-Sentinel*, 8 February 2000.

28 'Update on Miami-Dade/Monroe Corrective Action Plan', presented at the meeting of the State of Florida WAGES Board, 14 June 2000.

29 In a study of member concerns, workforce development was the number one concern of Florida's Chamber of Commerce members. See the Chamber's web site for further information at: (http://www.flchamber.com).

30 Targeted employer impact survey research conducted for *Workforce 2020*, as reported in Hudson Institute report, 'Workforce 2020: a local laboratory for business-driven reform', December 1999.

31 Targeted employer impact survey research conducted for Workforce 2020, as reported in 'Workforce 2020: a local laboratory for business-driven reform', 1999. See also data from the Florida Chamber of Commerce at: (http://www.flchamber.com/fba/welfare_to_work.asp).

32 General opinion research survey research conducted for *Workforce 2020*, as reported in Hudson Institute report, 'Workforce 2020: a local laboratory for business-driven reform', December 1999.

33 *WAGES Works Newsletter*, January 2000. For more information on The Jobs Partnership, contact The Mangum Group, P.O. Box 31768, Raleigh, NC.

34 Florida Department of Children and Families, as reported on the WAGES web site at: (http://www.wages.org/wages/fastfacts/fastfacts_flast.htm). The 81per cent reduction shows the number of families containing an adult. This number closely corresponds to the number of families subject to the WAGES time limit.

35 Crew Jr., R.E. and Eyerman, J., 'After WAGES: Results of the Florida Study', Florida State University, March 1999. Prepared for the Florida WAGES Board.

36 Crew and Eyerman, 'After WAGES: Results of the Florida Study', 1999.

37 'Qualitative study of WAGES draft final report', The Florida Inter-University Welfare Reform Collaborative, Autumn 1999.

38 See 'WAGES Employment Projects Initiative Must Address Its Design and Implementation Problems', OPPAGA Performance Review Report No. 99-21, December 1999. Specifically, this report says three major factors contributed to the lack of success of this programme: 1) diffused administrative responsibility for the initiative; 2) a short timeline for potential recipients to identify and develop projects for funding; and 3) unclear mission and purpose of the initiative.

39 'Board leadership 2000: the next agenda', Hudson Institute, Hillsborough Community College and Brandon Roberts+Associates, June 2000. Available on the internet at: (http://www.welfarereformer.org).

40 For a complete text of the bill creating Workforce Florida Inc., go to: (http://www.leg.state.fl.us/session/2000/Senate/bills/billtext/pdf /s2050.pdf).

41 WAGES Works Newsletter, January 2000.

42 See: (http://www.leg.state.fl.us/session/2000/Senate/bills/billtext/pdf /s2050.pdf).

43 See the Front Porch Florida, Office of Urban Opportunity web site at: (http://fcn.state.fl.us/org/frontporch).

44 See the Florida Commission on Responsible Fatherhood web site at: (http://www.fcorf.org/news.html).

45 See the Florida Commission on Responsible Fatherhood web site at: (http://www.fcorf.org/news.html).

46 Stephen Goldsmith's remarks at the Manhattan Institute's Center for Civic Innovation conference, 'Next Steps in Welfare Reform', 14 April 1999.

47 See the Florida Commission on Responsible Fatherhood web site at: ⟨http://www.fcorf.org/news.html⟩.

Milwaukee After W-2

Amy L. Sherman

The W-2 Revolution

Wisconsin is the nation's leader in welfare reform. Under Governor Tommy Thompson's radical reforms, state caseloads have plummeted a stunning 88 per cent, from just under 80,000 cases in 1994 to less than 9,000 today. 'Wisconsin Works', or W-2, is the pinnacle of Thompson's efforts. Established in 1997, W-2 has won praise from conservatives impressed with its tough 'work first' principles and from liberals lauding its generous and comprehensive benefits. Almost no one in Wisconsin, including the disabled, people with drug problems, and mothers of very young children, is exempt from working. Meanwhile, under W-2, the state is spending 45 per cent more per family than it did under the old Aid to Families with Dependent Children (AFDC) system. Yet, with the drop in the caseload, and privatisation efforts that save Wisconsin an estimated $10.25 million annually, W-2's aggregate costs are below what the state would have spent under the old system. No wonder policy makers of all stripes regularly make pilgrimage to the mid-west to see this thing which Wisconsin has wrought.

W-2's success will rise or fall on Milwaukee's experience, for there over 80 per cent of the welfare caseload resides. Reform critics predicted W-2 would spark disaster in the inner city. It hasn't. In the low-income Milwaukee neighbourhoods I studied, many poor families are faring better. Even more importantly, the long-term ripple effects of W-2

A shorter version of this essay appeared in *The Public Interest*, No. 140, (Summer 2000) pp. 36-48, 2000, by National Affairs Inc. Reprinted by permission of the author.

on families, community life, and the culture at large are promising. W-2 is simultaneously more rigorous, more complicated, more generous, more diverse, and more creative than the old welfare system. It offers much more than the traditional system, but also demands more—from the poor, from agency workers, and even from the non-profit social service sector. When W-2 works well, it is a vast improvement over the old, impersonal, inflexible AFDC system. The poor receive help individually-tailored to address their particular barriers to self-sufficiency. When W-2 case managers are competent, diligent, and kind, and W-2 recipients are motivated, attentive, and persistent, success reigns. When such qualities are absent from either, the resulting hardship can be severe. Much of the news from Milwaukee is good, and policy-makers outside of Wisconsin understandably want to replicate W-2 back home. But front-line poverty workers are identifying key points where the system's implementation isn't living up to its promise. If these constructive criticisms are erroneously dismissed as the laments of anti-reform liberals, friends of W-2 will miss a crucial opportunity to improve the programme—and preserve it from a backlash of antagonism produced by a few horror stories of human tragedy that could have been avoided.

How W-2 Works

Tired of a system in which counties held 'cost-reimbursement' contracts under which they received ongoing state funding regardless of their effectiveness in assisting people off the dole, the Thompson administration inaugurated 'Pay for Performance' in 1994. Under this initiative, counties could earn substantially more than their normal compensation if they achieved high job placement for welfare recipients, but had their pay cut for poor performance. The new regime resulted in a 30 per cent increase in job placements among welfare recipients in Milwaukee. W-2 built on the pay-for-performance concept and broke the counties' monopoly on welfare service delivery by opening up welfare administration to competitive bidding. In Milwaukee, five agencies—the for-profits Maximus and YW-Works and the

non-profit groups UMOS, OIC, and Employment Solutions
—competed for the right to serve their neighbourhoods and
were awarded contracts by the state totalling $357million.
Each agency oversees W-2 in a particular region of the city.
Milwaukee County did not contend for the opportunity to
administer W-2. According to researcher David Dodenhoff
of the Wisconsin Policy Research Institute, the state
discouraged the county from bidding because of its poor
record in administering the old system. Nonetheless, the
county remains involved in W-2. Its social workers are 'co-
located' with W-2 agency staff at jobcentres around the city;
they oversee food stamp, Medicaid, and daycare eligibility.

   Under W-2, needy individuals visit the job centre nearest
them. W-2 staff assess their work-readiness level, and
assign them to one of the system's four work categories. The
first tier is unsubsidised work. To avoid engendering
dependency, W-2 provides to applicants only as much
assistance as they need (the old system threw benefits
willy-nilly at people, sometimes killing them with kind-
ness). Called 'diversion' in the new vocabulary of welfare
reform, it means that staff encourage clients to accept
available full-time jobs through which they can provide for
themselves, rather than applying for government benefits
they may not need. Thus, applicants judged capable of
securing unsubsidised employment are merely given job-
search tips, help completing resumés and applications, and
leads to job openings. W-2 designers initially assumed that
only about 15 per cent of the caseload would be ready and
able to move immediately to unsubsidised employment;
encouragingly, as of December 1998, fully 31 per cent of the
caseload had been assigned to this first tier.

   The only problem is that some W-2 staff have been
overzealous about diversion. They have sometimes failed to
offer food stamps or childcare to clients who truly needed
them (and who, by getting this extra help in the short term,
could have been more successful in moving up to higher-
paying positions at their initial place of employment).
Liberals have enjoyed a heyday publicising the under-
utilisation of daycare, and, in May 1999, a US Department
of Agriculture report chastised a few of the W-2 agencies for

failing to give clients accurate information about food stamps and to process food stamp requests promptly. Under these pressures, agency staff are having to discern how to be faithful to W-2's philosophy of encouraging self-reliance while avoiding being negligent in providing participants with the services available to them. Walking that fine line is getting easier now, in that a greater proportion of applicants are from the most disadvantaged and dysfunctional of the poor. Thus, erring on the side of providing such applicants with a generous complex of assistance is considered justifiable.

Clients with few skills or spotty work histories are matched with a Financial and Employment Planner, W-2's version of the old caseworker, to assist them more intensively. Depending on their abilities, clients may be placed into tier two—'trial jobs' that last at least three months—or into tier three, longer-term, 'work experience' Community Service Jobs that combine work and training activities. As of December 1998, only one per cent of the applicants were placed into trial jobs and 51 per cent were assigned to Community Service Jobs. Clients with the most significant barriers to stable employment, such as substance abuse problems or mental illness, are placed in tier four, the 'W-2 Transition' category. There, they participate in work experience activities for 28 hours per week and engage in approximately 12 hours per week of education or training, for up to two years. As of late 1998, only 17 per cent of W-2 participants had been placed in this category, a lower number than the 25 per cent W-2 designers initially estimated. Today, though, as agencies reach down into the remaining portion of the welfare caseload where the hardest cases are, the percentage of applicants assigned to this tier is growing.

What's Happened In Milwaukee?

From the start, critics of W-2 worried it would inaugurate widespread homelessness and deepening poverty and hunger. But little evidence exists to support their worst fears. Data from food pantries, for example, is mixed.

Barbara Caravella of the Salvation Army's emergency services reports that their survey of city food pantries showed that about half saw an increase in requests for assistance while the other half saw a decrease. The Hunger Task Force of Milwaukee issued a study in late 1998 that suggested increased food insecurity among the poor and recounted instances of poor people digging through dumpsters or selling their blood plasma for money to buy food. However, only 30 per cent of the 632 individuals surveyed were active participants in W-2. Fifty-three per cent of W-2 participants said they were better off; for example, they were relying less on the school-based, federal free lunch programme for their kids than they had the year before. Mike Rintelman of the Milwaukee Outreach Center, a faith-based non-profit serving low-income and homeless families, says claims of increased hunger are ludicrous: 'the food pantries have surpluses'.

Data on evictions and homelessness are also slippery. Barbara Vanderburgh, Executive Director of the Joy House homeless shelter for women (the state's second largest facility) says thankfully: 'We haven't seen the apocalypse yet'. Rintelman's organisation claims a decrease in homelessness. Maria Rodriguez from the Milwaukee Housing Authority reports that there has not been a rise in evictions in public housing communities since W-2. Calls to the Salvation Army for rent assistance are, however, 'definitely up', according to Caravella. So are calls to A-Call, a special hotline for families faced with a housing crisis (97 families called in February 1998, and 236 called in October 1998).

William Martin, CEO of Employment Solutions, is reluctant to make a connection between W-2 and these increased calls for help. He points out that evictions in Milwaukee County have been steadily increasing for the last eight years, long before W-2 or Pay for Performance. Nonetheless, in December 1998, the Milwaukee *Journal Sentinel* carried a story entitled 'More women in shelters; group points to W-2'. It quoted homeless advocates and shelter directors asserting that W-2 was causing a rise in both homelessness and family break-up. Joe Volk, chairman of the Shelter

Task Force, described his staff's interviews with women seeking shelter:

> As we started talking to more and more of these so-called single women, we found they weren't single. They had children, and many of them had been sanctioned (penalized) by W-2 and had to place their children with friends or relatives while they went out on their own to try to re-establish some life.

Ken Schmidt, Director of the Hope House homeless shelter, added: 'I don't think anybody actually thought that W-2 was going to lead to parents having to give up their kids'. But Volk and Schmidt's statements blame 'the system' for the consequences of parents' irresponsible behaviour. If the moms had co-operated with W-2's work requirements, they would not have been sanctioned in the first place. Moreover, Charlene Hayes, the homeless woman featured in the *Journal Sentinel* article who had sent her children to live with relatives, had recently completed 90 days of detox in a substance abuse programme. Clearly, the primary cause of her homelessness and family breakup was not W-2, as the article asserted, but her drug problem. A March 1999 study of 62 homeless women, by the Center for Self-Sufficiency, further exposed the erroneous linkage between W-2 and homelessness. It found that W-2 'was *not* a major reason given by interviewees as a factor leading to homelessness. Only four respondents who were evicted and one respondent facing imminent eviction cited an AFDC or W-2 sanction as the proximate cause.'

Off to Work We Go

W-2's critics also worried that there would not be enough jobs for participants pushed into the labour market by the reforms. Not so, according to researcher John C. Weicher of the Hudson Institute. Instead, welfare rolls and unemployment have both gone down in Milwaukee. Using data from pilot studies produced by the Bureau of Labor Statistics, Weicher estimates that in May 1996 there were probably about 35,000 job openings with 30,000 people looking for work. In the last five years, unemployment in Milwaukee fell by 10,000 individuals, while the number of people working increased by 25,000. Today, unemployment stands at a mere 3.1 per cent.

The experiences of families from Hillside, a central city public housing community, strongly suggests a link between welfare reform and increased work. There, the number of households with at least one full-time income rose from 17 per cent in January 1996 to 55 per cent in January 1998. Data from other low-income city neighbourhoods show a dramatic increase in recent years in the number of single parents with dependent children filing income tax returns (up 31 per cent in the African-American community of Parklawn and up 40 per cent in the south-side Hispanic district) and massive increases in the aggregate amount of money returned to these low-wage workers through the Earned Income Tax Credit (up 176 per cent in Parklawn and 148 per cent in the Hispanic community). While these indicators do not prove that W-2 has more poor people working, they at least fit the hypothesis that more are.

Additional observations of and anecdotes from inner-city neighbourhoods support the claim that many aid recipients have moved from welfare to work. Nine months into W-2, for example, bus drivers working central city routes were seeing notable increases in passengers in early morning and late afternoon runs. 'I'm seeing different faces, more faces', said one in an interview with the Milwaukee *Journal Sentinel*. Another driver reported that he had more riders and that many were asking directions to various work sites. 'You kind of figure out that they're on W-2', he said. Sales of bus passes increased six per cent in 1998, Milwaukee Transit Authority marketing director Joe Caruso reported in the same article. 'We can't say that all's due to W-2, but we know a lot of it is, because social service agencies buy in bulk' for distribution to W-2 clients.

Moreover, since W-2, temporary agencies appear to be flourishing. The 1996 Milwaukee County yellow pages listed 175 temporary agencies; the 1999 yellow pages had 200. Tax preparation firms are also handling more business. Since 1996, H&R Block has opened five more branch offices in Milwaukee, Jackson Hewitt has opened one new location, and VIP Tax Service two. Faith-based groups operating used clothing centres report an increase in the number of individuals shopping for 'career clothes'. In the first five months of 1999, a record-number of 1,457 families visited the House of Peace clothing ministry. A volunteer named Shirley, who works in the 'First Impressions' section of the ministry, commented: 'There was lots of interest in [this section] right after W-2'. At least two new 'career-oriented' clothing centres have been established since W-2 to meet increased demand.

Other observations of neighbourhood business life also correlate with the claim that aid recipients are going to work. New daycare businesses are springing up, while established centres, like La Causa in the Hispanic district, have opened additional facilities. Perhaps in the hopes of capturing dollars from newly working W-2 participants, a new rent-to-own furniture company, Renter's Choice, has set up business in four locations city-wide. The pungent AP Foods Indian and Pakistani grocery on West Mitchell now boasts the tiny office of Amrit Patel's tax service. Joe Moftha of the B&S convenience mart on 12th and Concordia, a primarily African-American neighbourhood, has enjoyed about a $3,000 per week increase in gross sales in the past two years, and says it's because more of his customers are working. Before welfare reform, his business would boom during the first week of the month, as families received their AFDC cheques. After that, 'it would be dead almost'. Now, it's steadier. 'People are buying new cars and new clothes', Moftha said. 'I've seen a lot changing in the neighbourhood—people painting their houses and all that.'

Getting Behind The Numbers

W-2's critics rightly argue that evaluating the reforms simply by the number of people who exit welfare is insufficient—we need to know how those who leave fare. The available evidence is mixed, but more positive than negative. To show what was happening among families who left AFDC or W-2 between January and March 1998, Wisconsin's Department of Workforce Development released a 'leavers' survey in January 1999. It began the study after the caseload had dropped by 75 per cent, suggesting that its data reveals not only the experiences of the 'cream of the crop' recipients but of harder cases as well. Three hundred and seventy-five leavers were interviewed. Eighty-three per cent were found to have been employed since exiting welfare and 62 per cent were employed at the time of the interview. Of these, 80 per cent were working full-time at an average wage of $7.42/hour. Some leavers, like Alida Rodriguez, do better than this.

Rodriguez, a conscientious 26-year-old single mother with two young sons, has been promoted twice in her first year at the Latino Health Organization, Inc. At a full-time salary of over $18,000 annually, Rodriguez reports she is far better off now than when she was on welfare. 'I've been able to afford things that before there was no way I could buy', she says—like a 1979 Oldsmobile that has cut her morning commute from two hours to 30 minutes, Nintendo for her kids, and a used washer and dryer. 'I'm able to pay my bills on time. I pay my rent. I have enough for my lights and gas. And still I can go to the movies on weekends with the kids', Rodriguez smiles. 'I've seen a big change even though I don't get food stamps anymore and my co-pay[ment] for childcare has increased'. Rodriguez is helped by the fact that she still resides in subsidised housing, in Hillside. But she's hardly the only Hillside tenant doing better. Ricardo Diaz from the Milwaukee Housing Authority reports that the average income of Hillside residents has risen more than 30 per cent from January 1996 to January 1998.

African-American mom Michelle Crawford became W-2's best known success story when Governor Thompson invited her to address the state legislature as part of his 'state of the state' address. On welfare for ten years, Crawford admitted that when she first heard of W-2, she was scared. She was placed into a Community Service Job at the Engineered Plastics factory in Menomonee Falls. 'At first, they had me doing some housekeeping. I thought to myself, "What am I doing here? I could be doing this at home"', Crawford recalled. But she stuck with it and volunteered to complete additional assignments when other Community Service Jobs participants employed at the plant didn't show. Since her father had been a machine operator, Crawford was curious about work on the factory floor and asked her supervisor about the possibility of training for a machinist's position. The company agreed and Crawford began her training. 'I was so proud when I got the job', Crawford exulted. 'W-2 gave me a chance and I feel good about myself.' After a few raises, she now makes $11.50/hour.

James Taylor, Operations Manager at Family House, a faith-based non-profit providing nursing home care for low-income elderly residents of the Keefe Avenue neighbour-hood, has also witnessed welfare-to-work success stories. Family House's cook was on welfare two and half years ago. With five dependent children and no education beyond the tenth grade, 'she lived her life more or less day to day, dependent on the welfare cheque', recalls Taylor. With the advent of W-2's precursor, Pay for Performance, this woman approached Taylor for a job. 'She's been working for us for over two years now, and she's been saving her money', Taylor says. 'She used to live in a little seedy rooming house with all those kids. Now she's got her own flat. It's immacu-late. She comes to work every single day and wants extra hours when we offer them.' The cook says she is ecstatic about having control over her own apartment, since at the rooming house she shared the bathroom with strangers and would have to stand guard outside the door while her little girls used the facilities. Taylor recounts that for this woman, welfare reform 'kind of pushed her in the water and made her swim. So, there's good stories about W-2 out there.'

In late 1997, liberal authors Kathyrn Edin and Laura Lein published *Making Ends Meet*, based on interviews with welfare-reliant and working poor single moms in five cities. They calculate that poor single parents can 'make it' if they earn something over $8 an hour (about $16,000 a year). Many W-2 participants with full-time jobs come close. Eight I interviewed, who were currently working in full-time, unsubsidised jobs, had an average wage of $7.97 an hour. Maximus reports that its clients, in unsubsidised positions, average $7.46 an hour. Community Enterprises of Greater Milwaukee, a non-profit partnering with Employment Solutions, offers computer skills training to W-2 participants. Its graduates typically start at $8.00 an hour.

That's not exactly living high on the hog, so it may not be surprising that over 55 per cent of working moms interviewed in a survey by the Wisconsin Catholic Bishops reported that 'they worried a lot' about paying their bills. Nonetheless, according to calculations by Milwaukee's Center for Self-Sufficiency, a Wisconsin parent with two children who makes $8/hour will, with food stamps and the federal and state Earned Income Tax Credit, gross $19,647 annually. That's nearly $6,000 above the federal poverty level of $13,650 for a family of three. Apparently, W-2 is lifting many families above the poverty line, yet they continue to feel pinched. According to front-line poverty workers, the reason is that some newly working families fail to budget wisely. Maria Rodriguez of the Milwaukee Housing Authority reports that, since W-2, her agency has sent out more late payment notices, even though more public housing tenants are now working and achieving higher overall incomes. Her staff has met with families to discover the reasons for late payment—and poor budgeting is a major one. Under AFDC, women received a lump sum payment at the beginning of the month, from which they could pay their rent in full. Now they bring home a weekly or bi-monthly paycheque, not one of which is large enough to cover the rent. If they do not save a little from each paycheque towards rent, they can run short. Cordelia Taylor, executive director at Family House, has also observed W-2 parents running into budget problems. 'They feel that because the money is coming in more often, they can spend it more freely on wants instead of needs', Taylor says. 'Some of these young people are so in a hurry to have nice things. They don't want to go to a used appliance store. They say, "I've got this job and I want my friends to see me with my new stereo sitting in my living room". This is why it's so important for us to help people learn budgeting.'

Citing the surveys in which leavers express financial worries, reform critics tediously complain that W-2 has merely turned the welfare poor into the working poor. But surely it is unrealistic to think W-2 (or any other reform programme) could move participants miraculously from the poorest to the middle class—the journey is almost certain to include a stopover in the ranks of the working poor. More to the point, the working poor are better off than the welfare poor. They are almost always better off materially. Their participation in the labour force positions them for possible advancement. And it elicits greater sympathy from private charities and tax-payer funded programmes. After all, Americans are more likely to consider the working poor as 'deserving' of assistance.

W-2's Ripple Effects

W-2's positive impact on participants goes beyond economics, though. Almost all the W-2 participants I interviewed said that working had increased their self-esteem and their sense of hopefulness for the future. Another beneficial ripple effect of W-2 on low-income families is that it encourages the development of a more structured lifestyle through the discipline of the work-a-day world. 'Home life is getting more structured. It's 8.30—time to go to bed. It's morning—time to get up', Vicky Hill, Director of the King Day Care Center on Martin Luther King Drive, told the *Journal Sentinel*. According to Anthony Taylor of the Westside Housing Cooperative: 'Before, there were lots of people walking the streets at 11 or 12. Now, you see a thrust of people between 6 a.m. and 8 a.m. and again between 3.30 and 6 p.m. The kids seem better behaved, and there's less nuisance and truancy in the area.' Seeing mom go to work also has a positive effect on children's self-esteem, say youth workers like Shawn Bowen of the Parklawn YWCA. 'The kids are proud to see their mother[s] working.'

Kids aren't the only ones affected by mom's work—fathers and boyfriends are too. In some cases, mom's increased economic stability—and the boost that gives her self-respect—motivates her to throw out leeching boyfriends. In other cases, women who've taken jobs become more insistent that their boyfriends or children's fathers start pulling their weight—and that message is reinforced through W-2's expanded emphasis on child support enforcement and new programmes to help fathers get training and find employment.

W-2 also addresses one complaint raised by a welfare-reliant mother quoted in Edin and Lein's book, *Making Ends Meet*; namely, alienation from the mainstream economy. Indeed, integrating welfare recipients into the economy is one of the stated goals of W-2. Documents from Governor Thompson's office assert:

> Separating families in poverty from other economic classes isolates recipients from their communities. W-2 creates a true melting pot of job seekers from all economic levels and unites former welfare recipients with the rest of the unemployed population.

One of W-2's architects, Jason Turner, says simply: 'Work connects individuals to the larger society'. Observers have begun to notice this new integration. 'The AFDC world was very insular. I don't think people left their neighbourhoods much', said Nancy Nestler of Multicultural High School (which runs adult education programmes) in an interview with the *Journal Sentinel*. 'Now we're seeing a lot of mobility, people getting out more, families having a lot more exposure to services like counselling and parenting classes.'

W-2's work requirements also undercut the notorious 'crayfish syndrome' that plagued highly-motivated welfare recipients under the old AFDC system. Folk wisdom has it that if you put a bunch of crayfish in a bucket and one starts to climb out, the others will pull him down. A similar phenomenon sometimes confronted welfare recipients who sought to improve themselves. When public housing resident and welfare recipient Clarissa Crews set out to get her GED in the early 1990s, her neighbours harassed her. 'Who do you think you are? You think you're better than us?' Crews recollects their words with a grimace. Now, with W-2 essentially requiring all welfare recipients to better themselves, 'strivers' cannot be singled out for ridicule.

Troubled Cases

Not surprisingly, given the scope and scale of change W-2 has brought, alongside the success stories are credible stories of hardship. School officials complain that W-2 is taking a toll on children whose families bounce from one insecure housing arrangement to another. Marcus White of the Interfaith Conference of Greater Milwaukee, a network of churches and religiously-based social service providers, says he's heard dozens of stories of families having to double up to share expenses. School social worker Maxine Winston of Keefe Avenue Elementary says she's seen even worse: 'three or maybe four families living together in one house'. She adds, 'We're also watching fourth and fifth graders missing school to babysit sick younger siblings at home when mom can't find daycare and has to go to work'. That these troubling things are happening is indisputable. But the simultaneous existence of such suffering, and of the new W-2 system, does not automatically mean W-2 caused these hardships. Critics have been far too quick to note some painful problem, and then immediately point the finger at W-2. Such simplistic analysis won't move us forward in helping the people who need help, or fixing the parts of the system that need improvement. We've got to have a clearer understanding of who is suffering and why. Judging by interviews with strugglers, there are multiple reasons for hardship.

Causes Of Hardship

In some cases, the suffering is self-inflicted. That is, it results from the individual's failure to meet W-2's expectations. Examples abound. 'Elizabeth', a middle-aged resident at the Salvation Army shelter (known locally as the Lodge), admits she ended up homeless not from W-2 but from 'getting back onto drugs' and subsequently failing to fulfil the programme's work rules. Cynthia Donelson, a Parklawn resident who's been through a couple of Community Service Job placements, complains: 'I've been sanctioned plenty of times'. (The average sanction for W-2 clients in Milwaukee in 1998 was $336.) When I asked why, Donelson replied: 'I got kind of fed up with the system. Kind of got lazy'. She hated her first placement—at a factory—and sometimes just didn't show up for work.

Patricia Thompson, a social worker at the Lodge, sees self-inflicted suffering often. 'I just got a call from a young lady

[who] had an appointment to go to see her worker over at YW-Works', she told me in a representative anecdote. 'Well, she didn't go because she didn't have transportation, she didn't have anybody to keep her kids, she didn't have any money. She didn't want to take all her children with her. I understand that, but I said "You need to go". Now she doesn't have any money and she's not going to get any [assistance] for three months. So here she sits getting ready to be evicted—three kids, 18 years old—and doesn't know what in the world to do. Now that is really her fault, in a sense, because she didn't get there [to her appointment]. And then she waited until the last minute to try to call and get somebody to do something for her,' Thompson says in exasperation. 'So it's not that all of them in here [at the Lodge] are victims of the system. And not all the ones in the community are either, because I can tell you, just with the referrals I got this week, there must be 15-20 [people] that did not do what they were supposed to do.'

Other individuals are suffering because they were impatient with the new system and gave up on it too quickly. They had one negative interaction with agency staff, got disgusted, abandoned W-2, and attempted to find a job on their own. For some, the end result was tolerable; others experienced disaster. Pauline Nash is bitter about her short-lived experience on W-2. Her family hit a crisis in 1998 when her unemployment ran out and her husband was temporarily unable to work. 'I didn't know how I was going to pay my rent, my lights, my gas. My kids didn't have anything to eat', Nash remembers. 'So I went down there [to the W-2 agency] to get help and they made me feel so bad. They told me I'd have to work 55 hours before I could get a cheque or emergency food stamps. It was crazy!' This should not have been Nash's experience—emergency food stamps are available immediately when appropriate—but it may have arisen because the system's emphasis on diversion discourages staff from offering instant help. On the other hand, Nash ought not to have waited to ask for help until the last possible moment. In any event, she abandoned the thought of getting aid from W-2 and begged Cordelia Taylor for a job (who not only offered one but also gave her some groceries to tide the family over). Some of Nash's friends who tried to make it on their own did not fare as well. She knows three who gave up on W-2—too much red tape—and sought help from temporary agencies. Six months later, one was working at Kentucky Fried Chicken, one at Family Dollar, one as a security guard in the mall—all making minimum wage. The woman at KFC, who has four kids, fell behind on her rent, got evicted, and had to move in with the Nashes for a few weeks.

Then there are those who have suffered hardships that could have been avoided if they, or agency workers, had communicated better. Before she got on the road to success, Alida Rodriguez floundered in her first two interactions with her assigned W-2 agency. Unhappy with a Financial and Employment Planner (FEP) who 'treated me like a number' and a system where 'everything was very confusing', Rodriguez dropped out of W-2. For seven months, she tried to work as many hours as possible through temporary agencies, and did not apply for food stamps or Medicaid because she didn't understand that she could still receive them without participating in W-2. Maxine Winston says she knows of many stories like this and criticises the agencies for not clearly explaining the eligibility rules for benefits. Former AFDC recipient Judie Eschrich has flourished in her job at Amerivoice, a small telephone service company, having worked her way up in nearly two years to the CEO's 'right-hand woman'. But she failed to report her new job at Amerivoice to the County agency overseeing her rent assistance. 'I thought it was intertwined with W-2 and they'd know I was working', Eschrich says. The result: her budget was crunched by having to pay back $1500 in rent assistance overpayments.

Still other W-2 participants suffer because of shortcomings by agency and county employees. Ruby Rodriguez had been staying at the Salvation Army Lodge for 20 days when I met her in late April 1999. An articulate Latino woman with a high school degree and five children under age 13, Rodriguez spent an hour describing the run-around she was getting at her assigned W-2 agency. 'I'll go down there, wait for two or three hours, and finally talk to a guy. He'll give me some job listings and tell me I have 72 hours—three days—to find a job. When I get one I should let them know, and then the childcare will be provided', she explains. 'But after I get a job, I'll get a letter saying my daycare has been denied. So then I can't find anyone to watch my two youngest ones, and so I'm jumping from job to job. And I'd go back to the W-2 agency and ask, "Why am I being denied?" And they'll say, "Ms. Rodriguez, you're not participating correctly". But I tell them, "I am participating, I'm trying to co-operate."'

Complaints And Their Legitimacy

Rodriguez' two main complaints—an incompetent and inattentive FEP and screw-ups with her daycare benefits—have legitimacy. Patricia Thompson and other social workers outside the W-2 agencies emphasise the huge role played by FEPs in the lives of clients—some going so far as to say that a client's success in W-2 depends primarily on the competency of the FEP. From her multiple interactions with agency staff, Barbara Vanderburgh of Joy House says simply: 'Some FEPs are fantastic, others, jerky'. Fortunately, she reports, 'the majority seem to do a decent job'. W-2 agency staff admit, though, that in the early days, FEPs were handling case loads of 120 to 130 clients—well above the 55 client-per-caseworker guideline suggested by W-2's designers. With such high caseloads, some W-2 participants were bound to get short shrift.

In recent months, W-2 agencies have established new customer service procedures to address problems of miscommunication and poor treatment. YW-Works has installed a phone system that tracks how often FEPs log into their voice mail; FEPs are required to return their calls within 48 hours. YW-Works has also established a customer care call-in centre where participants can get their general questions answered even without talking to their FEP. Agencies are also limiting their FEPs' caseloads. At Maximus, FEPs take on no more than 75 clients. 'We want to give our customers more personal attention', says an agency spokeswoman. But, as 75 clients per FEP is still a larger caseload than W-2's designers originally thought appropriate, the agencies need to go even further.

The daycare glitches Ruby Rodriguez related were not the fabrication of a disgruntled welfare recipient. They were embarrassingly frequent in W-2's early days. Richard Buschmann, Director of Childcare for Milwaukee County Department of Human Services, admitted in October 1998 that 'glitches' had arisen in as many as 60 per cent of the daycare cases in W-2's first six months. Clients eligible for help were wrongly denied benefits, and childcare providers often did not receive timely payment from the county. That led to some providers refusing to serve W-2 participants, for fear they wouldn't get paid—creating an obvious headache for single moms rushing to comply with W-2's work requirements. Childcare administration was so poor that eventually the state took over this responsibility. This appears to have improved things: childcare providers I spoke with in June reported that they were receiving correct and timely payments and knew of few W-2 participants with continuing daycare hassles.

W-2 does have a formal grievance process in place. Clients can complain to their FEP's supervisor and, at some agencies, enter a mediation process. Most problems are cleared up at this level. If not, clients can file for a 'fact finding' procedure—and if this fails to bring satisfaction, the state will conduct a formal hearing. The good news is that, as agencies have gained experience in administering W-2, the number of fact findings has decreased. The bad news is that, though sometimes clients' complaints are discovered to be unfounded, the statistics show that slightly more often their grievance is proved and agencies are found negligent. According to state records, in the final quarter of 1998, 72 grievance cases got to the hearing stage. Thirty-nine decisions (54 per cent) were made in favour of the client and 14 (19 per cent) in favour of the agency. The remaining 19 adjudications (26 per cent) were classified as 'other'; here the decision represented some sort of compromise between the two parties. In the first quarter of 1999, 191 fact findings were conducted for Milwaukee. Most concerned complaints of unfair sanctions or payments problems; a few involved daycare glitches. In 31 per cent of the fact findings, the agency's action was overturned in favour of the client; 22 per cent of the time the agency decision was upheld. In all other instances, the cases were withdrawn by either the client or agency or some compromise was fashioned.

The Need For Hand-holding

For W-2 to become the nation's most successful reform initiative in lifting the needy out of poverty, administrators will not only need to get errant case workers in line or fine-tune the eligibility and sanctions processes so that needy individuals are neither wrongly denied help nor penalised unfairly. They will need to avoid a blind devotion to the system's personal responsibility message that prevents them from acting realistically towards the remaining, hardest-to-serve, segment of the caseload.

W-2, which is both more demanding and more rewarding than the old welfare system, is working well for clients who pay attention to details, stay organised, and are diligent, patient, and thick-skinned. But not all clients currently possess these strengths; indeed, fewer and fewer in the bottom tier of the welfare caseload do. Many cannot inter-face effectively with the bureaucracy. They may be illiter-ate, have a poor command of English, or be unable to organise themselves and all the necessary papers—birth certificates, medical records, paystubs, agency letters, and benefits applications. Under AFDC, welfare recipients could be more passive: they attended a couple of meetings, answered a few questions, filled out some forms—and month after month, their aid cheque appeared. W-2 demands that they be active participants in shaping their own road to self-sufficiency. They must attend more meetings, must com-plete a minimum amount of job-search activities (recording their visits and phone calls to potential employers and reporting back to the agency), and, if they want to gain the most from the agency, must actively inquire into the wide range of services available to them (such as literacy and budgeting classes, transportation assistance, loans for job-related expenses, and membership in a 'job club', to name a few).There is more documentation to stay on top of and more appointments to keep—with significant penalties for non-attendance. There's nothing inherently wrong with all this. But without a lot of hand-holding, the nonchalant, the timid, the slow-to-understand, the young and clueless, and the touchy and impatient, will not succeed in this system. So, W-2 administrators can choose. They can legitimise hand-holding, and risk being called spineless by ideological purists who see this as countering the personal-responsibility message of W-2. Or, they can permit a lot of poor people to fail, and thus risk being called heartless by the left.

In making their choice, policy makers would do well to heed the advice of front-line, pro-reform poverty workers like Deborah Darden. She is the Executive Director of 'Right Alternatives', the programme Marvin Olasky, author of *The Tragedy of American Compassion* and strong national advocate for work-based welfare reform, has publicly and heartily commended. Darden got herself off welfare by eschewing the entitlement mentality, accepting personal responsibility for her circumstances, working hard, and relying on God. Then she began helping others in the Parklawn project to do the same. For nearly ten years she has run support groups emphasising personal responsibility and traditional values, and she has established a neighbourhood centre to provide training and daycare. Darden's complaints about W-2, in short, do not come from a welfare defender.

Darden says the country needed welfare reform and work requirements. Nevertheless, she emphasises: 'There is so much in the details of the suffering of the people that is not being [publicised]. Everyday I'm getting calls for help. I've known people—good people, good workers, not the kind who had to be pried out of their seats—who've got caught up somehow and have been evicted, homeless!' In fact, she says, these have included some of the very same women touted by Olasky. Darden would like to see welfare reform's two-year time limit extended for individuals with legitimate hardships, and thinks the W-2 agencies need to do more outreach and home visits, patiently explaining the system's procedures to clients who feel overwhelmed and confused by the changes. She favours the establishment of incentive programmes under which W-2 participants who are faithfully complying with work requirements could also attend college and have their tuition reimbursed by the state if they maintain a 'B' average. And she says the agencies need to crack down on businesses that are taking advantage of W-2 workers. For example, she relates stories of W-2 participants who, at the encouragement of their W-2 agency, have accepted private sector jobs in suburban companies, with disastrous consequences. The firms have abruptly shifted the women's work schedules—wreaking havoc on their carefully designed daycare and transportation plans. They have promised the women full-time hours but delivered only part-time hours, creating financial crises. Company staff have failed to submit crucial reports back to the W-2 agencies concerning the work records of W-2 employees—resulting in unfair sanctions.

Darden argues that too often, once the W-2 participant is placed in a job, caseworkers at the agencies fail to monitor her circumstances, leaving her unprotected against businesses that 'jerk her around'. In some instances, Darden knows of women who've quit such jobs and feel they cannot return to their W-2 agency (for fear of being criticised). To make ends meet, such women work in the informal—or illegal—economy. 'We have people who don't use drugs selling them to make ends meet. W-2 people are selling drugs, selling themselves, selling food', Darden laments. 'People are having to get imaginative with hustling, with "where can I get money from?" Come back and talk to me in five years,' Darden intones darkly. 'If we're not putting safety nets in place, if we're not looking at the kinds of support systems people are going to have to have, I know crime is going to go up. Absolutely.'

Darden's views are shared by Cordelia Taylor of Family House and Bill Locke of Community Enterprises. 'A lot of these [W-2 participants] have never seen anybody who worked before', Taylor says. 'They don't understand how to get themselves ready for work, how to be here on time—even why it's important to be on time. One young lady said to me one time: "You are yelling at me for just being late two or three times this week!" And she said it with a straight face. She just didn't understand.' Bill Locke explains that the harder-to-serve clients now on W-2 come from a 'very disoriented, disorganised society. They're not conditioned to any kind of formal lifestyle.' He is supportive of W-2 and very critical of the old welfare system, but wishes more welfare reform supporters would embrace the necessity—and legitimacy—of mentoring and one-on-one support. Taylor concurs. 'People say to me, "But you're holding people's hands, and they have to learn to make it on their own". That's true. But [hand-holding] has to be done if we're going to make a success out of this W-2.'

Taylor has had to fire about half of the dozen W-2 participants she has employed at her complex of low-income nursing homes. 'Part of the problem that I'm finding as an employer is that I'm spending so much time teaching these young women basic things', she says. 'You know, how to prepare the children for school the night before—how to braid the hair, tie it down, put the cereal in the bowls and cover it with a paper towel so that in the morning you'll only have to pour the milk.' When she teaches young W- 2 mothers such simple 'life lessons', they look at her in amazement. '"Oh, I hadn't thought about that!" they'll say.' Taylor—who sees herself first as a Christian minister and second as an employer—is willing to take time to impart these kinds of life skills. But she wishes the W-2 agencies would do more of it, so that W-2 participants would be better prepared for the workplace.

The Key To Success

If the experiences of the W-2 'success stories' I interviewed are illustrative, they support the contentions of Darden, Taylor, and Locke. For in every instance, these W-2 participants credited their success to the personal, caring support they received from someone who helped them walk the road from welfare to work. For some, the extra help came from family. Alida Rodriguez says she would have been homeless during her seven months off W-2 if her mother hadn't babysat her kids for free. For others, it was an agency staff member who went the extra mile. Churches or faith-based non-profits helped others to make it. Pauline Nash chokes up while relating Cordelia Taylor's kindnesses. Lewanna Alexander, a W-2 participant flourishing in her Community Service Job at Vieau Elementary School, says she'd still be a drug addict if it weren't for the storefront church that rescued her, housed her for months, and helped her navigate the W-2 process.

For still others, it was the employer who made the difference. Judie Eschrich is grateful that the CEOs of Amerivoice stuck with her despite her inexperience and offered her flexi-time so she could attend mandatory W-2 appointments. 'In the beginning, I was just sort of *duh*—I couldn't figure anything out!' Eschrich laughs. Yet, her boss was patient, and even brought in clothes for Eschrich's kids. Alida Rodriguez and other W-2 participants working at the Latino Health Organization expressed fervent gratitude for its Executive Director, Maria Gamaz. Gamaz takes the praise in her stride; she doesn't see the extra hand-holding she does—such as interceding with the W-2 agencies—as charity, but as good business. 'I place a call. I get it resolved—and here's a happy, smiling, productive employee', Gamaz says. 'If you offer supports, if you invest, let these workers know that they have opportunities, then they feel hope and they give 100 per cent.'

Exporting W-2

Judging by the enhanced supports W-2 agencies have erected in recent months for clients in the remaining 20 per cent of the caseload, it appears that they are heeding the advice of friendly critics like Darden and Taylor. Maximus, for example, has instituted a wake-up call programme where job retention specialists telephone clients during the first few weeks of their new job to help ensure they get to work on time. YW-Works bought its own factory, Generation

Two Plastics, so that it could run its own on-the-job training centre for unskilled W-2 participants. All of the agencies are exploring partnerships with faith-based groups specialising in drug rehabilitation, soft-skills training, and mentoring. Neighbourhood associations and homeless shelters report with satisfaction that they're seeing an increase in W-2 agencies sending outreach workers to meet with low-income families on-site. These attempts to go the extra mile in reaching the most disadvantaged and dysfunctional low-income families are critical to W-2's success in Milwaukee—and any other city where it is tried.

W-2's strong work-first message is laudable. Its assumption that the needy themselves, and not government, are responsible for their own well-being is indisputable. Its penalties for non-compliance are tough, but not immoral. In short, the system's rules and expectations need little adjustment. Pragmatism and grace, though, are necessary to its success in Wisconsin or anywhere else. 'We're going to have to start to meet people where they *are*, not where we assume they *should be*', Cordelia Taylor emphasises. 'These young women are lost and need individual assistance.' As Deborah Darden sums up, 'It's not about "babying". It's about being realistic.'

Welfare Reform: Four Years Later

Douglas J. Besharov
and Peter Germanis

In August 1996, a Republican Congress pushed a reluctant President Clinton to sign a bill that ended welfare as we had known it. But since the 1996 welfare reform act expires on 30 September 2002, its eventual fate is not yet clear. Much will depend on how the law's impact is viewed. So far, it certainly seems to be a success. By June 1999, welfare rolls had fallen an amazing 49 per cent from their historic high of five million families in March 1994. That's nearly seven and a half million fewer parents and children on welfare.

It has suited the purposes of both the Clinton administration and the Republican Congress to claim that 'welfare reform' has caused this dramatic decline—and that over two million former recipients are now working because of the new law. But that's not quite true. The strong economy —and massively increased aid to the working poor—almost certainly have had more impact than welfare reform per se. Moreover, as many as 40 per cent of the mothers who left welfare are not working regularly but are instead relying on support from boyfriends, family members or friends, and other government and private programmes.

Both liberals and conservatives have found it convenient to ignore this reality—conservatives because it gives the 'Clinton economy' and the president's success in expanding aid to the working poor too much credit and Republican welfare reform too little, and liberals because it suggests

This essay is reprinted with permission of the authors from *The Public Interest*, No. 140, (Summer 2000) pp. 17-35, 2000, by National Affairs Inc.

that many welfare recipients didn't 'really need' government benefits. But the failure to be clear about why the rolls have declined so much prevents an accurate accounting of the law's impact—and what needs to be done next.

Welfare's Rise And Fall

For nearly 60 years, it seemed that welfare rolls could only grow. With the exception of a few short-lived declines, the rolls grew from 147,000 families in 1936 to about five million in 1994, from less than one per cent of all American families with children to about 15 per cent.

Between 1963 and 1973, there was a striking 230 per cent increase—not because of a bad economy (unemployment was actually quite low during most of this period) nor simply because of an increase in family breakdown (both divorce and illegitimacy were rising, though not nearly as fast as the welfare caseload). Rather, the increase was largely the result of programmatic changes that made it easier for income-eligible families to get benefits, as well as the destigmatisation of being on welfare. Where once welfare agencies discouraged applicants (by pressing them to seek other means of support or by imposing a gruelling eligibility process), the obstacles to enrolment were now lowered. New York City's rolls almost tripled in only five years (between 1965 and 1970) under liberal mayor John Lindsay. The same liberalisation was taking place across the nation, as welfare came to be seen more as a 'right' than as a temporary safety net. Some of the drive behind this national movement was undoubtedly the long-overdue repeal of Jim Crow-like rules in the South that kept African-American mothers off welfare.

After this liberalisation, caseloads stayed roughly steady for almost 15 years. They rose again, by 34 per cent, between 1989 and 1994, largely because of the weak economy. But there were other important causes: a spike in out-of-wedlock births among some groups; an increase in immigrants applying for means-tested benefits, either for themselves or their American-born children; half-a-decade's outreach efforts to get single mothers to sign up for Medicaid (and thence welfare benefits); and an increase in child-only cases, perhaps as a result of the spread of crack addiction among mothers and an increase in cases of parental disability.

Regardless of what caused rolls to rise in the past, they rarely fell back very far. Thus no one predicted the recent halving of welfare since 1994. Fifteen states have had declines of over 60 per cent; three report declines of 85 per cent or more. Indeed, almost everywhere, welfare rolls are way down and work is way up. For example, never-married mothers, the group most prone to long-term welfare dependency, were 40 per cent more likely to be working in 1999 than in 1994. What's responsible for the decline in welfare and the increase in work?

The End Of Welfare As We Know It

In 1992, Barbara Sabol, then New York City's welfare commissioner, visited two of her own welfare offices dressed in a 'sweatshirt, jeans, and scarf or wig'. She told the welfare workers she needed a job in order to care for her children. But try as she would, she could not get the workers to help her find a job.

The same year, candidate Bill Clinton showed that he was a New Democrat by ambiguously promising to 'end welfare as we know it'. After the election, his administration granted many state waivers that, among other things, toughened work requirements and imposed partial time limits on benefits—ultimately culminating in the Republican-inspired 1996 welfare reform law.

The Republican bill bore a superficial resemblance to what Clinton proposed, so both sides were able to claim credit for reforming welfare. But the changes in welfare were largely based on the Republican plan. While both bills imposed time limits on benefits, the Clinton proposal included an entitlement to a public job afterwards. The Republican bill had no such entitlement, and also transformed the programme into a capped block grant, which gave states an incentive to cut caseloads because they would get to keep any unexpended funds.

Today, Sabol would find that welfare workers are eager to find jobs for their clients. Across the nation, the culture of welfare offices has changed—from places where mothers are signed up for benefits (with almost no questions asked) to places where they are helped, cajoled, and, yes, pressured to get a job or rely on others for support. The US General Accounting Office described the change this way:

Under states' welfare reform programs, participation requirements are being imposed sooner than under JOBS [the old welfare regime], with many states requiring participation in job search activities immediately upon application for assistance. Before reform, recipients could wait months—or even years—before being required to participate, and many never were required to participate because of the lack of sufficient services and staff.[1]

Many welfare offices are now 'job centres', where workers help applicants and recipients find employment. Depending on the office, they teach how to write résumés and handle job interviews; provide access to word processors, fax machines, telephones, and even clothes; offer career counselling and financial-planning services; and refer applicants to specific employers with job openings. In a survey of former welfare recipients in Texas who left the rolls in December 1996, over 60 per cent said the welfare agency 'gave me the kind of help I needed'.

Some of this is boosterism, plain and simple, with welfare workers giving young mothers the moral support they so often need. As one caseworker said: 'Some of these women never thought that they could get a job. We give them the confidence to try'. But the assistance also can be quite concrete. Besides large expansions in Medicaid and child-care, many states provide cash assistance to families on welfare to help them leave or stay off. These payments range from a few hundred dollars to over $2,000. For example, Texas provides stipends to help such families pay for employment-related expenses, such as transportation, education, and training. Virginia gives transportation allowances for up to a year after leaving welfare. And about a dozen states have created or expanded EITC-like tax credits for low-income families which can be used for any purpose.

In a real break from the past, however, few welfare agencies seem to put any stock in job training. Administrative data from the states indicate that less than two per cent of adult welfare recipients are in some sort of formal job-training programme. Instead, agencies emphasise immediate job placement and on-the-job work experience. This gives mothers much-needed work experience, but it also adds to the pressure they feel to leave welfare or not apply for it in the first place. For there is also a sharper edge to welfare reform.

In most places, the welfare application process has a new element: 'diversion'. Diversion is a straightforward effort to keep families off welfare. It is encapsulated in two simple questions now asked of welfare applicants: Have you looked for a job? Can someone else support you? Many welfare agencies maintain a bank of phones that applicants must use to call as many as 20 potential employers before they can even apply for benefits. When told of these requirements, many applicants simply turn around and walk out.

In New York City's 'Job Centers', for example, all applicants are encouraged to look for work (and offered immediate cash support for childcare) or to seek support from relatives or other sources. Those who still decide to apply for welfare are required to go through a 30-day assessment period during which they complete the application process and undergo a rigorous job-readiness and job-search regimen involving many sessions at the Job Center and other offices. At the end of this period, eligible able-bodied adults who choose to receive assistance are required to participate in the city's workfare programme. As a result, New York City officials estimate that the percentage of mothers entering these Job Centers who are eventually enrolled has fallen from about half to about a third of applicants.

The Hassle Factor

Being on welfare has also changed, but not as much as many people think. When welfare reform was being considered by the Congress, most analysts expected the states to establish large, mandatory work programmes in order to satisfy the bill's 'participation' requirements. However, because those requirements were set in relation to 1995 caseloads, the sharp decline in the rolls since then has obviated the need for such programmes—and few places beyond Wisconsin and New York City have established them.

Instead, almost all states require recipients to sign 'self-sufficiency agreements' describing their plan for becoming self-sufficient within a specified time frame. Iowa, for example, requires all able-bodied recipients without infant children to develop and sign a Family Investment Agreement. Failure to sign or comply with this agreement can result in immediate and complete termination of cash assistance. About ten per cent of those who begin this process seem to have their benefits terminated for failure to sign or comply with the agreement.

In addition, most states now impose various behaviour-related rules. Parents are required to have their children immunised and to send them to school; in a few places, mothers and fathers must even attend family or parenting skills classes. Failure to comply with these requirements can result in the welfare grant being reduced—and, in about 37 states, even terminated. According to state administrative data, in 1998, 6.2 per cent (or 180,000) of the 2.9 million families that left welfare did so after a sanction. In some states, the percentage was as high as 30 per cent.

These and other new requirements raise what economists would call the 'cost' of being on welfare. By a rough calculation that assumes recipients value their time at the minimum wage, these kinds of requirements can reduce the advantage of being on welfare versus working by about 50 per cent. In very low-benefit states, the advantage can fall to zero.

This amounts to the reintroduction of a long-gone aspect of being on welfare, 'hassle'. And it clearly leads some welfare recipients to seek other ways of supporting themselves. When these new requirements are explained to applicants and recipients, they often say things like: 'I guess I might as well get a real job' or 'I might as well move back home.' Or they just walk out of the office—or stop responding to warnings that they will lose their benefits if they do not participate in work-related activities. In the 1996 Texas survey of former recipients, about a quarter said that important factors for leaving were either 'unfriendly caseworkers' or 'new programme requirements'. And in a survey of those who left welfare in South Carolina between January and March of 1997, 60 per cent said they felt 'hassled', and 13 per cent said that is why they left. About a third said that the state's welfare programme 'wants to get rid of people, not help them'. A similar survey was conducted in Wisconsin for those who left welfare in 1998, and the results were about the same. (Of course, hassle may have led others to leave welfare, though they cited some other reason, such as finding a job.)

These are dramatic changes in welfare, and it is natural to assume that they are responsible for recent caseload declines. But welfare reform has coincided with the strongest economy in at least three decades, coupled with an unprecedented increase in aid to the working poor. The increased returns for low-skilled work are probably as responsible for the decline in welfare, and perhaps more so.

Work Pays

The strong economy, most experts agree, has played a key role in the welfare declines. The rolls started falling in 1994, two years before the enactment of the 1996 welfare law, and before the welfare waivers that allowed some states to 'get tough' on welfare recipients could have had much impact. The weak economic conditions that helped drive up welfare rolls during the Bush presidency ended a few months before George Bush left office (not soon enough, of course, to affect the election). Since January 1993, the economic news has been truly remarkable: real per capita Gross Domestic Product up about 25 per cent in real dollars, 20 million new jobs, the highest ever employment-to-population ratio (64.3 per cent), and the lowest unemployment rate since 1970 (4.1 per cent).

Most relevant to the welfare decline has been the increase in average real earnings, especially among low-wage workers. For example, since the second quarter of 1996, weekly earnings for full-time workers have grown 5.3 per cent. The gains for low-income, full-time workers have been even larger: 7.0 per cent for those at the twenty-fifth percentile of earnings and 8.5 per cent for those at the tenth percentile of earnings.

Also helping to reduce caseloads has been the progress in fulfilling Clinton's promise 'to make work pay'. Both Democratic and Republican Congresses have supported (the latter sometimes reluctantly) Clinton's initiatives for massive increases in government aid to the working poor. So much so that this spending now far exceeds what was spent on the old AFDC programme. Between 1993 and 1999 alone, total aid to the working poor increased by about $25 billion a year, from about $40 billion to about $65 billion (in 1999 dollars). At its height, combined federal and state spending on AFDC never exceeded $30 billion.

The Earned Income Tax Credit (EITC), for example, provides a cash subsidy to low-income, working parents. Between 1993 and 1999, total expenditures on the EITC rose from $18 billion to $30 billion (all in 1999 dollars). The increases for particular groups were striking: for example, the income supplement for a single mother (with two children) working at the minimum wage more than doubled, rising from about $1,700 to about $3,900 per year.

Childcare aid has also expanded, becoming all but an entitlement for those families leaving welfare. Total annual federal and related state childcare expenditures rose from $8 billion to over $12 billion in the same years, providing childcare slots for well over one million additional children. Gaps in coverage remain, and take-up rates may be lower than many advocates say are appropriate (although the latter is probably because so many parents already have access to government subsidised childcare or have other family members who can care for their children). In any event, subsidised childcare is obviously helping many low-skilled and low-earning mothers work.

Medicaid eligibility, too, has been substantially expanded. While Medicaid was once limited primarily to families receiving welfare, sequential expansions for pregnant women and children (beginning in the mid-1980s) have taken eligibility to between 100 and 250 per cent of the poverty line (depending on the child's age and the state programme). The welfare-reform law gave states authority to expand coverage for adults, and some have done so. As a result, total Medicaid and related healthcare costs for low-income families with children rose from $15 billion in 1993 to $24 billion in 1999—making millions more children (and sometimes families) eligible.

The absence of healthcare coverage is not an insuperable barrier to work for mothers who are healthy and who have healthy children. But for those mothers who have chronic illnesses, or whose children have them, the threat of losing coverage can be a substantial disincentive to leaving welfare.

Clinton also managed to push through the Republican-controlled Congress a two-stage increase in the minimum wage—from $4.25 an hour to $4.75 an hour on 1 October 1996, and then to its current $5.15 an hour on 1 September 1997. Moreover, additional expansions in aid to the working poor are looming. The child tax credit and Child Health Insurance Program will grow as they are fully phased in. The Clinton administration has proposed further expansions in childcare and the EITC, and has taken steps to expand participation of low-income working families in Medicaid and food stamps. It also continues to push for increases in the minimum wage.

Explaining The Decline

A number of respected researchers have used econometric models to estimate how much of the caseload decline was caused by welfare reform itself compared to the economy and increased aid to the working poor.[2] The models they use, unfortunately, are extremely sensitive to the assumptions and variables incorporated, making their findings imprecise. Nevertheless, most of the studies lead to a similar conclusion: in the early years of the caseload decline (1994–96), around 40 or 50 per cent of the decline was due to the economy and the stronger job prospects for low-skilled workers. Later in the economic expansion (1996–99), the same and other studies conclude that the economy accounted for only about ten or perhaps 20 per cent of the decline.

Many studies also attempt to gauge the impact of the increased aid to the working poor. This decade-long effort to 'make work pay' may be an even more important factor in the declining rolls, accounting for perhaps 40 to 50 per cent of the initial declines and 30 to 40 per cent of the later declines.

As for welfare reform itself, these studies usually estimate its impact at from 15 to 20 per cent for the early declines and about 30 to 40 per cent for later ones. (Most studies also find that the failure to increase welfare benefits, a 20-year trend, reduced rolls another five to ten per cent.) Consolidating the estimated impacts on initial and later declines (and weighting them for the size of each), here is what the studies suggest: the robust economy explains 15 to 25 per cent of the decline; aid to the working poor 30 to 45 per cent; increases in the minimum wage zero to five per cent; and welfare reform 30 to 45 per cent.

Having too much confidence in the results of such econometric models is always questionable. These studies have many weaknesses, including the failure to include all policy changes, such as heightened child-support enforcement. Most also fail to consider at least partially independent demographic factors, such as declines in out-of-wedlock births, drug abuse, crime, and immigration. We doubt, for example, that increased aid to the working poor has had as much impact as they suggest; we would attribute more of the decline to the strong economy and to welfare reform generally. Nevertheless, these studies were carefully conducted, and their results are roughly consistent. Thus it seems reasonable to conclude that they correctly reflect the approximate contribution of these four factors to the decline in caseloads.

It is possible that welfare reform has played a more substantial role, interacting with the strong economy and more generous aid to the working poor to encourage more single mothers to try working. By this way of thinking, the strong economy and more generous aid are necessary but not sufficient conditions—with welfare reform providing the needed motivation for people to seek jobs or the support of others who have jobs. After all, we have had strong economies in the past without concomitant welfare declines; sometimes welfare rolls have even risen. In other words, the impact of each of the factors may be greater than would otherwise be the case if they had occurred alone.

The results of randomised welfare experiments, however, seem to confirm econometric estimates of welfare reform's only partial role in reducing caseloads. Starting in earnest in 1992, states were granted waivers from the old AFDC rules, but only if they established rigorous, random-assignment experiments to measure the impact of their new policies. Many of these new policies bear a close resemblance to the programme restrictions in new-style state welfare regimes, such as tougher work requirements, time-limited benefits, family caps, and linking benefits to immunisation and school attendance. The experiments also reflect many of the expansions in benefits that characterise welfare reform, such as liberalised resource limits, transitional benefits, eligibility for two-parent families, and earnings disregards (which allow working recipients to keep more of their benefits). About ten of these experiments have yielded findings that provide an indirect measure of welfare reform's impact on caseloads.

Across all ten of these waiver studies, and regardless of the varying combination of programme components, the difference between the experimental and control groups is rarely more than a few percentage points. The biggest declines in welfare receipt due to welfare reform do not exceed 15 per cent or so, often over two or three years. This does not mean that welfare reform's contribution to the decline is only 15 per cent. We recognise that these randomised experiments are an imperfect measure of welfare reform's potential impact because they do not capture either its role in discouraging people from going on the rolls ('entry effects') nor its broader impact on personal and agency behaviour (partly through a change in community values). The point is that no rigorously evaluated programme of welfare reform has ever had an impact even remotely comparable to what has happened to national welfare caseloads.

Indeed, sometimes the group receiving the 'reformed' welfare services was less likely to leave the rolls. This is because most of the waiver experiments, like most state-implemented welfare reforms, include components that both decrease caseloads (like work mandates) and increase them (like the expansion of earnings disregards). Thus Minnesota's 'welfare reform', which expanded the state's earnings disregard, asset limits, and two-parent eligibility for benefits, while imposing modest work requirements, increased caseloads by almost five per cent for long-term recipients after 21 months.

Leaving Welfare Without Working

In addition to the often unappreciated contribution of the economy and aid to the working poor, another significant aspect of the caseload decline is that so many mothers seem to be leaving welfare without taking jobs.

The best source of data about the families that have left welfare are surveys of former welfare recipients ('leaver studies') that have been conducted by various states and by the Urban Institute.[3] Although they all have some weaknesses, such as low response rates and insufficiently detailed information, the best studies tell about the same story: between 60 to 70 per cent of those who left welfare were employed at the time they were surveyed (and 60 to 85 per cent had been employed at some point since leaving). Of those who were working, about 60 to 80 per cent seem to work full-time, earning about $6 to $8 per hour (or about $800 to $1,000 per month). The remainder worked fewer hours and thus earned less money. (Many studies, however, exclude the 20 to 30 per cent of leaver families that returned to welfare, which tends to minimise the difficulty some mothers have finding work.)

Broader measures of employment are consistent with this high level of non-work among leavers—and also suggest that many of the single mothers who did not go on welfare are also not working. For example, between March 1994 and March 1999, the number of employed single mothers with children under age 18 increased by 1.251 million (from 5.712 million to 6.963 million). During the same period, welfare caseloads (almost all including a single mother) fell by 2.430 million (from 5.098 million to 2.668 million). Even if the entire 1.251 million increase in the number of single mothers working in this period represented those who were previously on welfare (or would have gone on welfare during the period), they would still amount to only about half of the caseload decline.

Some mothers who left welfare, of course, may not be reporting their employment. A four-city study conducted by researchers Kathryn Edin and Laura Lein in the early 1990s found that about 30 per cent of low-income working mothers and about 50 per cent of welfare mothers had unreported work.[4] But there is no reason why the percentage not reporting work should have grown in recent years. If anything, the expansions in earnings disregards and the EITC should have encouraged more low-income mothers to report their employment.

Thus, only about 50 to 60 per cent of the mothers who have left welfare (and stayed off) seem to be working regularly. The surprisingly large number of mothers leaving welfare without then working has been all but ignored by most commentators, including severe critics of welfare reform. Yet this has profound implications for the economic and social condition of low-income families.

Other Sources Of Support

How could so many mothers have left welfare without working? Work requirements and heightened levels of 'hassle', by lowering the value of welfare, would be expected to cause mothers to leave welfare for work, even relatively low-paid work. But why would mothers leave welfare without having a job? The burdens placed on them hardly seem sufficient reason for them to abandon their only support for themselves and their children.

The leaver studies suggest the answer: these mothers have other sources of support besides welfare. In South Carolina, for example, non-working leavers were almost twice as likely as working leavers to have other sources of support—including other forms of government assistance, such as Social Security (13 per cent *vs.* six per cent) or Supplemental Security Income (20 per cent *vs.* eight per cent); free housing from a parent or relative (15 per cent *vs.* 10 per cent); another adult in the home to help with the bills (17 per cent *vs.* seven per cent); and help from someone outside the home (22 per cent *vs.* eight per cent). A study of former recipients in Milwaukee, conducted by the Hudson Institute and Mathematica Policy Research, found that over two-thirds of all the mothers who left welfare received help (e.g., transportation assistance, a place to stay, and food) from family or friends. Those leavers who were not working were about 15 per cent more likely to be receiving such help (72 per cent *vs.* 63 per cent).

Most leaver studies do not identify the sources of support for working and non-working mothers separately, but they do reinforce the importance of other household members or income sources. In Iowa, after families were dropped from welfare, they were about 33 per cent more likely to be relying on others for a place to stay (25 per cent *vs.* 33 per cent). Similarly, in Florida, where families have begun to lose welfare due to a time limit, one-third of those who hit the time limit either moved or had a different living arrangement, such as adding another household member to help with the expenses. Finally, in Connecticut, 43 per cent of the families that left welfare due to the state's 21-month time limit reported living with at least one other adult six months after benefit termination. (There is no comparison data for the period before the time limit was reached.)

When welfare reform was being debated, many experts predicted increases in such 'co-residency' or doubling up arrangements as mothers were pushed off welfare. So far, however, there is little evidence of substantial increases in co-residency (or marriage, for that matter). According to Christopher Jencks, for example, the total number of single mothers residing with another adult has remained essentially stable since 1988, with no discernible change after welfare reform. It is possible that many mothers entered such living arrangements while their total number remained constant—with as many mothers having left such arrangements because of the improving economy, as entered them, because they were pushed off welfare. But without more data, it is impossible to know for sure.

There is another way that mothers can leave welfare without working: they can fall back on pre-existing co-residency arrangements (together with other sources of support). Based on a study by Rebecca London, which used data from the Survey of Income and Program Participation, we calculate that, in 1990, before the declines in welfare caseloads, at least 37 per cent of welfare mothers lived with other adults—18 per cent with their parents, six per cent with a boyfriend, and 13 per cent with others.[5]

These findings may seem surprising, but for many years now the welfare system has largely ignored the household income in such co-residency arrangements. Depending on the situation, the income of the grandparents, with whom the adult welfare mother was living, would not be considered (for example, if the mother was an adult herself); and the man-in-the-house rule (which denied benefits to households with a cohabiting male) was abandoned years ago. We would suggest that when faced with the new work and behavioural requirements, mothers who had other sources of support sufficient to permit them to forgo welfare (predominantly those living in households with adequate economic resources) simply left welfare without looking for work.

It also helps that many of these mothers are still receiving other government benefits—primarily food stamps and housing—which are often much more valuable than the basic welfare payment. (The continued availability of Medicaid also encourages mothers to leave welfare without finding work, even if the family does not sign up for coverage until someone is taken ill.) Non-working mothers on their own could not subsist on only these benefits, but non-working mothers living with others (or getting support from others) could get by.

This is in particular the case in low-benefit states where it may simply no longer 'pay' to be on welfare as opposed, say, to food stamps. In Alabama, for example, in 1999, the welfare benefit for a family of three was just $164 per month, compared to a food-stamp allotment of $329. (Moreover, the food-stamp benefit comes with virtually no strings attached, whereas cash assistance can be accompanied by work and other behavioural requirements that reduce its value still further.) So mothers in low-benefit states can leave welfare and not suffer anything like a complete loss of income, especially if there are other adults in the household that have income.

This makes economic sense. If one assumes that these mothers value their time at the minimum wage or above, then there is little incentive for them to engage in work activities for 20 to 30 hours per week to avoid a sanction that can be as little as $10 to $50 per week. The added income from complying with these requirements translates into an effective wage of 50 cents to two dollars per hour. This does not compensate for the lost free time (what economists call 'leisure') that mothers can use, for example, to care for their children or take a job with unreported income. Data on this behaviour are difficult to obtain, but its possible magnitude is suggested by the following: between 1994 and 1998, the number of single-parent families on food stamps that were both not on welfare and with no earnings grew by 10 per cent, or 55,000 families. While this is an imperfect measure, it could easily understate the phenomenon.

The economy and aid to the working poor could also play a role here, as more households would become economically comfortable enough for the mother to leave welfare without working. This would be consistent with earlier patterns. Greg Duncan of Northwestern University and his colleagues used data from the Panel Study of Income Dynamics (PSID) to determine why mothers left welfare between 1986 and

1991.[6] (Leaving welfare was defined as receiving welfare in one year but not the next year.) They found that about one-half of welfare exits were for work (or a rise in earnings), about a quarter for changes in marital status or living arrangements, about five per cent because there were no children under 18, and the remainder were due to a variety of reasons such as an increase in other transfer income or a change in state of residence. About one-third of the earnings-related exits involved an increase in the earnings of an adult already in the household other than the mother, demonstrating the importance of shared living arrangements.

These dynamics also explain the behaviour of those mothers Larry Mead of New York University calls the 'happily sanctioned'. Such mothers accept less in welfare benefits rather than work or meet other behavioural requirements. In about 14 states, which include about half the national welfare caseload, the sanction for non-compliance is only a partial reduction in benefits—that is, the family's grant is reduced by some per cent, usually representing the mother's share of the grant (about one-third of the welfare cheque). These mothers may not actually be happy, but since this reduction typically amounts to only one-sixth of the mothers' total package of benefits, one can see why they willingly make the trade-off.

Assessing 'Welfare Reform'

When congressional Republicans were pushing for the enactment of their welfare reform bill, opponents predicted widespread hardship—including sharply increased homelessness. Happily, there is no evidence that welfare reform has caused substantial increases in homelessness or other indicators of extreme hardship, such as foster-care placements or substantiated reports of child abuse and neglect. And despite extensive efforts, journalists have found few individual horror stories of the harmful effects of welfare reform. As one administrator said: 'We underestimated their ability to get jobs that meet their basic needs—or to get support from other sources'.

For a while, it appeared that incomes of the poorest single mothers might be edging down—a sign that welfare reform might be squeezing those at the bottom. A widely disseminated study by Wendell Primus of the Center on Budget and Policy Priorities estimated that, from 1995 to 1997, the bottom quintile had experienced an eight per cent drop in income. Even though many of these mothers were not welfare leavers (nor likely to have gone on assistance before welfare reform), advocates latched onto this income decline as a sign that welfare reform should be reconsidered. However, Primus' further analysis after another year of data has reduced the estimated income loss for this group to about four per cent. In the same period, 1995 to 1998, all the other quintiles of income for single mothers rose, with the middle quintile up seven per cent, going from $20,617 to $22,063.

But if welfare reform has not been the social catastrophe some predicted, neither has it lifted large numbers of female-headed families out of poverty. Thanks to the EITC and other aid, most of the mothers who left welfare and are working now have more income than when they were on welfare. But average earnings are only about $12,000 a year. And as we saw, many mothers simply left welfare—without working. Unless they lived with someone or moved in with someone earning a great deal more, they probably suffered at least a partial loss of income.

Moreover, some of those who gained income through work may not be immediately better off. They also have more expenses. Even if their childcare costs are fully covered, they still face other work-related expenses, such as transportation and clothing. And by working, they lose the ability to earn additional money off the books. Thus their higher income comes at the price of having to work many hours a week while also raising their children, often on their own.

There are many weaknesses in the data that underlie the foregoing conclusions. For example, it is very difficult to find and count the number of homeless families and individuals, much less get detailed information on their characteristics. Data on substantiated cases of child maltreatment are a function of the number of reports received, the ability of the system to investigate them, and the willingness of states to report them. Even the much-cited income data used to measure trends in financial well-being are plagued by numerous problems. Perhaps most significantly, reported welfare receipt in the Current Population Survey (CPS) is over one-third lower than indicated by administrative records, a problem that has been worsening in recent years. These surveys also miss much of the income that is earned working 'off-the-books' or received from boyfriends or other household members. For example, recipients may want to conceal this income from those administering the survey, for fear that it could affect their eligibility for welfare.

This mixed picture of life after welfare is captured in the 'before and after' questions asked in six of the more reliable leaver studies (Mississippi, New Mexico, South Carolina, Virginia, Washington, and Wisconsin).[7] Depending on the study, between 20 and 40 per cent of those responding said that 'life was better' while on welfare. Conversely, 60 to 80 per cent of former recipients think that life is the same or better being off welfare. (Three states asked separately about being better off. In all three, about 55 per cent said they were 'better off'; about 25 per cent said they were doing the 'same'; and about 20 per cent said they were 'worse off'.)

What should we make of these patterns? First, reducing welfare rolls is a tremendous and unprecedented achievement—especially given the apparently small amount of additional hardship. If this result had been guaranteed when welfare reform was being debated in 1996, most opposition would surely have melted away. Indeed, even some past opponents of welfare reform have been quieted by its apparent early success. Nevertheless, welfare reform should not be given credit for the consequences of a stupendous economy and unprecedented increases in aid to the working poor. More of the mothers who gained ground after leaving welfare can probably thank the latter two factors for their improved situation, and more of those who lost ground probably left assistance because of welfare reform and the added hassle associated with it.

What about those mothers who are now working but not making much more than their previous welfare benefits, or those who are now relying on the support of others rather than welfare? Robert Haveman, an economics professor at the University of Wisconsin-Madison, says that they are 'treading water, but staying afloat'. We hope they are not just treading water, but building their skills or living in households where the prime earner is doing so.

For most Americans, welfare reform was not just about reducing the rolls, nor was it some silver bullet that would immediately eradicate poverty. Instead, it was about reducing the deep-seated social and personal dysfunction associated with long-term dependency, thereby ultimately reducing poverty. For welfare reform to be a success on this measure will depend on whether the low-paying jobs taken by many leavers lead to better jobs, whether the household arrangements (and other sources of support) that have allowed mothers to leave welfare without working prove supportive and nurturing, and whether the eventual result is less dysfunctional behaviour among parents and better outcomes for children. We may need a generation to find out.

Notes

1   US General Accounting Office, *States Are Restructuring Programs to Reduce Welfare Dependence*, Washington DC: US General Accounting Office, June 1998, p. 38.

2   Council of Economic Advisers, *Explaining the Decline in Welfare Receipt, 1993-1996*, May 1997; Martini, A. and Wiseman, M., *Explaining the Recent Decline in Welfare Caseloads: Is the Council of Economic Advisers Right?*, Washington DC: The Urban Institute, 1997; Figlio, D. and Ziliak, J., 'Welfare Reform, the Business Cycle, and then Decline in AFDC Caseloads', prepared for presentation at the conference, Welfare Reform and the Macroeconomy, Washington DC: October 1998; Wallace, G. and Blank, R., 'What goes up must come down? Explaining recent changes in public assistance caseloads', prepared for the conference, Welfare Reform and the Macroeconomy, 1998; Council of Economic Advisers, *The Effects of Welfare Policy and the*

Economic Expansion of Welfare Caseloads: An Update, 3 August 1999; Dickert, S., Houser, S. and Scholz, J., 'The earned income tax credit and transfer programs: a study of labor market and program participation', *Tax Policy and the Economy*, 9, 1995, pp.1-50; Page, M., Spetz, J. and Millar, J., 'Does the minimum wage affect welfare caseloads?', a working paper by the Joint Center for Poverty Research, September 1999, www.jcpr.org/wpfiles/Page_WP.pdf

3   US General Accounting Office, *Welfare Reform: Information on Former Recipient Status*, Washington DC: US General Accounting Office, April 1999; Brauner, S. and Loprest, P., 'Where are they now? What states' studies of people who left welfare tell us', *New Federalism: Issues and Options for States A*, No. 32, Washington DC: The Urban Institute, May 1999; Loprest, P., 'Families who left welfare: who are they and how are they doing?' *Assessing New Federalism: Discussion Papers*, Washington DC: The Urban Institute, 1999.

4   Edin, K. and Lein, L., *Making Ends Meet: How Single Mothers Survive Welfare and Low-Wage Work*, New York: Russell Sage Foundation, 1997, pp. 150-51.

5   London, R., 'The interaction between single mothers' living arrangements and welfare participation', *Journal of Policy Analysis and Management*, 19, No. 1, 2000; and personal communication from Rebecca London, 5 April 2000.

6   US Department of Health and Human Services, Office of Assistant Secretary for Planning and Evaluation, *Indicators of Welfare Dependence: Annual Report to Congress*, Washington DC: US Department of Health and Human Services, October 1998, Table IND 8b.

7   Beeler, J., Brister, B., Chambry, S. and McDonald, A., *Tracking of TANF Clients: First Report of a Longitudinal Study: Mississippi's TANF State program*, Jackson, MS: 28 January 1999, revised; MAXIMUS, *New Mexico Longitudinal Study: Results of the First Year Follow-Up Survey*, Washington DC: MAXIMUS, 14 April 2000; South Carolina Department of Social Services, Office of Program Reform, Evaluation, and Research, *Comparison Between Working and Non-Working Clients Whose Cases Were Closed Between January-March 1997*, Columbia, SC: South Carolina Department of Social Services, 12 March 1998; South Carolina Department of Social Services, Division Program Quality Assurance, *Survey of Former Family Independence Program Clients: Cases Closed During January Through March 1997*, Columbia, SC: South

Carolina Department of Social Services, 1997; Kuhns, C., Gordon, A., Agodini, R. and Loeffler, R., *The Virginia Closed Case Study: Experience of Virginia Families One Year After Leaving Temporary Assistance for Needy Families*, Falls Church, VA: Center for Public Administration and Policy, Virginia Polytechnic Institute and State University, 12 November 1999; DSHS Economic Services Administration, Division of Program Research and Evaluations, *Washington's TANF Single Parent Families After Welfare: Management Reports and Data Analysis*, January 1999; State of Wisconsin, Department of Workforce Development, *Survey of Those Leaving AFDC or W-2 January to March 1998 Preliminary Report*, Madison, WI: Department of Workforce Development, 1998; and Swartz, R., Kauff, J., Nixon, L., Fraker, T., Hein, J. and Mitchell, S., *Converting to Wisonsin Works: Where Did Families Go When AFDC Ended in Milwaukee?*, Madison, WI: The Hudson Institute and Mathematica Policy Research, Inc., 1999.

New York Reformed
How New York was Transformed from US Welfare Capital to Reform's Epicentre

Jay Hein

Introduction

There is nothing more difficult to plan, more doubtful of success, nor more dangerous to manage than the creation of a new order of things....Whenever his enemies have the ability to attack the innovator they do so with the passion of partisans, while others defend him sluggishly, so the innovator and his party alike are vulnerable.

Niccolo Machiavelli, The Prince

With these words, Machiavelli's counsel ought to have sounded cautionary to New York mayor Rudolph Giuliani in his pursuit of creating a new order of welfare provision in one of the world's largest cities. For it was the city of New York that gave birth to the welfare state expansion movement ignited by the Great Society politics of the 1960s, and it was there that the most severe poverty and social exclusion gained seemingly near permanent residence.

Because he is a consummate politician, it is likely that Giuliani was aware of Machiavelli's teaching. Even if not, it probably would have had little effect on the mayor's announcement on 20 July 1998, to '... end welfare [in New York City] by the dawn of the new century'. To make his aspirations clear, Giuliani further said: 'We will replace dependency with work in exchange for earnings'.[1]

Giuliani had no obvious political motivation in assuming such a substantial risk. For starters, he was already immortalised for having stemmed the wave of crime that had previously earned New York the reputation as one of

America's most dangerous cities. During Giuliani's first half-dozen years in office, crime fell by 50 per cent and murder by an astonishing 70 per cent. The New York mayor's record of welfare reform was almost as impressive. Between 1995 and 1998, Giuliani created the largest local welfare-to-work programme in the nation, involving over 30,000 participants at any point in time during this period. By the time of his speech in July 1998, his administration's workfare initiative had moved over 400,000 people off the welfare rolls. This number of former welfare recipients was larger than the total number of residents in any other city in the state of New York, and it exceeded the total welfare escapees in Wisconsin, a state nationally renowned for its welfare reform success.*

Such heralded social policy success would lead most public officials to rest on their laurels, so why did Giuliani go one step further to join Wisconsin governor Tommy Thompson as the only officials attempting to completely replace welfare in their domains? In his own words, Giuliani said it was because of his compassion for the poor, and his impatience with so-called progressive politicians whose policies led to doling out welfare benefits to one in seven New Yorkers without asking anything in return. 'The politicians and political theorists who supported increasing dependency facilitated the deterioration of thousands of families,' said Giuliani.[2]

War On Poverty Ground Zero

Such strong words would be unfriendly to many who supported expansion of the social reforms of President Lyndon Johnson's Great Society initiative. But nowhere could the call be more unwelcome than in New York, the birthplace of the welfare rights movement of the 1960s. At centre stage of this drama was the National Welfare Rights Organization (NWRO), founded by George Wiley in New York in 1966. At its zenith in 1969, NWRO membership was

---

*   However, Wisconsin's over 90 per cent reduction is
     certainly a percentage decline far beyond that of any
     other city's or state's experience.

22,000 families nationwide with local chapters in nearly every state and major metropolitan area.[3]

Established as an attempt to link the newly forming anti-poverty cause to the civil rights movement, the NWRO organised tens of thousands of welfare recipients to demand cash assistance, clothing, and food for their families. It was this effort more than any other that infused black women, who comprised over 90 per cent of NWRO's membership, with the belief that welfare was an entitlement not an act of generosity. NWRO provided training that 'taught women to claim their dignity and respect by insisting that society has a responsibility to care for children, and that women raising children on welfare had the right to determine how to spend their benefit cheques on their children's behalf'.[4]

The NWRO also helped fuel the early feminist movement in the United States, notably through NWRO president Johnnie Tillmon's essay, 'Welfare is a woman's issue', published by Ms Magazine. Tillmon's argument was that women possessed a right to adequate income, regardless of whether they stayed at home to raise their children or held down a job. She further explained that 'being on welfare was a necessity created by the economic system, not the fault of individual women—and that surviving on welfare was a badge of honor, not a symbol of shame'.[5]

The welfare rights strategy, led by the NWRO and allies such as the authors of Poor People's Movements, Frances Fox Piven and Richard Cloward, was both a smashing success and inglorious failure. During the Kennedy and Johnson administrations, the welfare rolls in New York tripled from 250,000 in 1960 to over 800,000 in 1968. Between 1968 and the mid-1990s, the number of welfare families in New York would never drop below 800,000 on any given day.

The welfare expansion's dark side was sadly evidenced by the increasing levels of poverty that accompanied the families who settled for a welfare cheque rather than a job, and by the intergenerational welfare dependency that followed. These negative results were unintended, to be sure, but a very real burden to the families caught in the poverty trap and to the city that housed them.

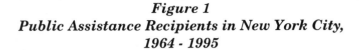

Figure 1
Public Assistance Recipients in New York City,
1964 - 1995

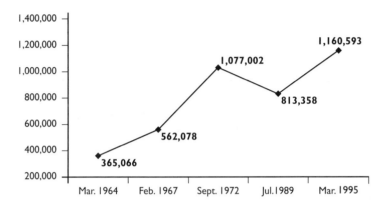

Source: NYC Human Resource Administration.

In his July 1998 welfare replacement speech, Giuliani reminded listeners that it was none other than Robert F. Kennedy (President Kennedy's brother and eventual US senator from New York) who refused to equate compassion with dependency, as it removed the poor from the essential economic and civic commerce of society.[6] Indeed,

[Robert] Kennedy's clearest difference with mainstream liberal opinion was over welfare. Unlike conservatives, who opposed federal spending for the poor, Kennedy criticized welfare on the grounds that it rendered millions of Americans dependent on handouts and thus unable to play a role in democracy.[7]

Giuliani shared that sentiment, and he initially turned to another Democratic standard-bearer, Franklin Delano Roosevelt, for an example of how to re-engage the poor back into the economic and social mainstream. In the earlier part of the century, President Roosevelt fought back against the Great Depression by launching the Work Progress Administration (WPA). Under New York mayor Fiorello LaGuardia's leadership, the WPA employed 700,000 New Yorkers in just seven-and-a half years. LaGuardia aimed to not just keep these men busy, but also utilise the WPA rebuild and modernise the city. In fact, WPA projects accounted for more than half of all construction in the city, and it included such self-named projects as FDR Drive and LaGuardia Airport.[8]

It was this spirit that Giuliani sought to rekindle when he became the city's mayor in 1992 and established what would become the largest workfare programme in the nation. By the end of his first term in office, there were 30,000 New Yorkers who cleaned city parks and provided other services in exchange for their welfare cheques and another 400,000 people who left the welfare rolls, a group larger than the population of any other city in the state of New York.

Beyond Workfare

Successful by relative standards, Giuliani realised that his workfare initiative lacked profound and systematic change. It was one thing to enhance the incentives and support structure to help the more motivated recipients help themselves, but a far more aggressive approach was needed to help those who faced significant barriers to self-sufficiency. Enter the mayor's challenge to engage all New York welfare recipients in meaningful work activity by the dawn of the new century (read: a mere 18 months following his July 1998 speech).

Even more dubious than Giuliani's bold proclamation to end welfare as New Yorkers knew it, was his choice to carry out such a vital mission: the much-maligned 13,000-person Human Resources Administration (HRA), an agency oft characterised as the most troubled welfare operation in the nation. New York Times writer Jason DeParle emphasised this point in a December 1998 article where he described the city's welfare caseworkers as '... rigidly clerical and chronically discontent'. To underscore his assessment, DeParle described one welfare office that had five per cent of its staff on worker's compensation benefits, nearly all for injuries sustained while falling out of a chair.[9]

This feeble agency is the horse Mayor Giuliani would ride into battle in his attempt to replace welfare in America's toughest laboratory. Notably, the mayor chose a new field general to sit atop this horse to wage war with the bureaucracy as well as the anti-reform forces that stood in the Administration's path. Giuliani selected Jason Turner, who served as one of the chief architects of Wisconsin's first-in-the-nation welfare replacement programme, and who considers work the pre-eminent solution to whatever ails low-income families.

Upon assuming control of the HRA, Commissioner Turner immediately took his message to the frontline staff who were used to hearing political sloganeering, only to keep doing business as usual. Turner quickly disabused them of the notion that Giuliani's charge was mere rhetoric by regaling staff with speeches that emphasised that work is the best training programme, not to mention the best antidote to drug abuse, depression, or other demons that plague New York's poor.

Turner acknowledges that his fascination with poverty reform dates to a 1 November 1965 US News and World Report article entitled 'How It Pays to Be Poor in America'. The article pointed out that for the eight million Americans on public assistance, idleness paid almost as much as working at a low wage. An accompanying text box illustrated all that the government gave away at the time—cash, food, housing, schooling—and predicted a growing 'welfare society' in the United States.[10]

As a 12-year-old in Darien, Connecticut, Turner had previously never thought that whole classes of citizens would be excluded from society by choosing to live off the government rather than support themselves and their families through work. The sixth-grade Turner designed his first welfare-to-work scheme—factories that would put these welfare dependents to work—in the pages of his middle-school notebook.

According to Turner: 'What liberals have entirely failed to grasp is that social maladies, including poverty, are the result of learned behavior in which enforced idleness is a contributing factor'.[11] Further, Turner believes that: 'Work is one's own gift to others, and when you sever that relationship with your fellow man, you're doing more than just harm to yourself economically. You're doing spiritual harm'.[12] These sentiments parallelled the growing opinion in America that work was key to one's well-being and social inclusion, echoing Robert Kennedy's words three decades ago. However, Turner's own words were harsher than Kennedy's, which incited critics to claim that he lacked compassion.

In January 1998, the month he named Turner to head HRA, Giuliani confirmed his resonance with Turner's philosophy by proclaiming in his State of the City address that: 'We will establish a work requirement for everyone receiving benefits. Other than for severe disabilities, there will be few exceptions.' Not surprisingly, Giuliani cited Turner's success in Wisconsin as a leading credential influencing his appointment. Said Giuliani: 'He's put an emphasis on moving people who were previously on welfare to work ... and of changing welfare from a welfare program to a work program'.

As welfare chief, Turner formed a team of senior advisers who shared his views and possessed complementary skills sets. Among them was New York University political scientist Larry Mead, who was hired as an external consultant to HRA for evaluation and work programmes counsel. Dr Mead is the author of numerous books and articles extolling the virtues of work requirements in welfare programmes. One such strategy pertained to the front door to welfare assistance, which Mead believes should be narrower to allow only the truly needy in. Explains Professor Mead: '[Diversion] is certainly not the intention to turn away those who need aid, but rather to make sure that people don't apply for aid casually'.[13] In what could be described as the anti–welfare rights strategy, diversion worked as advertised. Early in Turner's first year as HRA commissioner, welfare application approval rates nose-dived by 50 per cent at local offices.

Another key adviser brought to New York by Turner was Andy Bush, who was hired from the Hudson Institute, where he served as the think tank's Madison, Wisconsin, office director and founding director of its Welfare Policy Center. Bush and Turner collaborated on Wisconsin's welfare reinvention project in the mid-1990s. Bush was well-known for his promotion of the family-strengthening provisions of the 1996 federal welfare reform law, the topic of a paper he co-authored with National Fatherhood Initiative president Wade Horn. The central tenets of Bush's pro-marriage argument stemmed from mounting evidence that illegitimacy was the leading contributor to poverty in America. The mayor's office concurred that such family issues mattered to welfare reform, and a speech was drafted for the mayor in the spring of 1998 calling illegitimacy the number one threat to the future of New York City.[14] Such sentiment was virtually lifted from the Hudson paper on fatherhood and marriage, wherein Bush and Horn argued that: 'There is no greater threat to the long-term well-being of children, our communities and our nation, than the increasing number of children being raised without a committed, responsible and loving father'. This type of moralistic talk was uncharacteristic of the mayor, who tended to talk of virtue sans family-values rhetoric.

However, the mayor never delivered the speech. After a draft of the remarks was leaked to Newsday, the paper derided the pending speech as more of the Murphy Brown-bashing* that embroiled former vice president Dan Quayle in a family-values controversy that caused many to think Quayle was out of touch with modern America. Giuliani blinked, and the speech was later given with eloquent lines

---

* Murphy Brown was a fictional television character who proudly chose to give birth out of wedlock, proving to TV viewers that a woman could have a successful career and family life regardless of marital status. In a national speech on the importance of family values, then Vice-President Dan Quayle criticised the *Murphy Brown* episode as evidence that Hollywood was betraying the sanctity of the American family. Barbara Dafoe Whitehead later defended Quayle's position in an *Atlantic Monthly* cover story titled 'Dan Quayle Was Right', which prompted the issue to become the third best-selling in the magazine's history and led then-President Bill Clinton publicly to concur with Dafoe Whitehead's premise.

describing the re-moralisation of work, but silence over the re-moralisation of the family.

Implementation

The Human Resources Administration, with professionalism, accountability and integrity, will create lasting improvements for individuals and families in need, so they may attain their maximum degree of self-reliance. By doing so, we will enhance the quality of life for all New Yorkers.

HRA Vision Statement, 1998

It is one thing to start a revolution, and quite another to successfully implement one. HRA leadership took the mayor's July 1998 speech and created a new vision statement followed by an aggressive effort articulating its meaning to all staff in the 28 local offices and preparing them to fulfil their tasks. The sense of urgency did not come from City Hall alone. The 1996 federal welfare law required states to engage the majority of their caseload in work activity, or suffer severe financial penalties. Further, the new law placed a five-year time limit on the receipt of cash assistance for welfare families.

Thus, HRA's mantra became: the law has changed; each centre needs a plan; and each plan needs to be implemented. To help develop these new plans and build muscle tissue to execute them properly, a heavy emphasis was placed on training staff. Town hall meetings were held for all 18,000 staff, including welfare, housing, and medical services. Then a team of consultants, led by Peter Kaiser (another successful Wisconsin welfare-to-work veteran), translated the new vision into centre operations.

US management expert Stephen Covey has remarked that all organisations are perfectly aligned to get exactly what they are getting. This was certainly true of the HRA field offices, which the Kaiser Group found to be in serious disarray due to an unco-ordinated strategy of simply adding programmes on top of each other over many years. Suffering from a top-down, one-size-fits-all approach, as well as the power of multiple unions, centre managers did not have any clear lines of responsibility.

During the Great Society years, centre managers could be best described as working supervisors. Kaiser's goal was to first help them grow into managers and ultimately into leaders. To do so, he helped the central office transform itself from a command-and-control enterprise into a leadership organisation. Kaiser taught HRA leadership that their customers were the field staff, whose customers were the programme participants. This philosophy was manifested in the central office's speedy response to local agency needs, such as fixing copying machines to prevent unnecessary delays. Kaiser consultants observed some cases where only one of the agency's 12 copiers was operational. In the past, the situation would have lingered while mid-range bureaucrats sought approval for the repairs, but now such matters were deemed mission-critical to their agenda and quickly resolved.

Figure 2
New York's New Management Paradigm

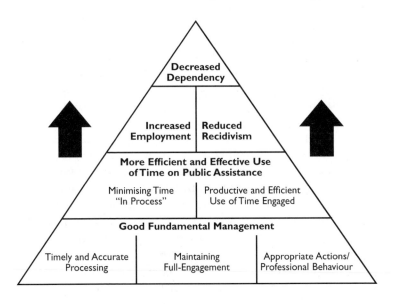

Source: NYC Human Resources Administration

Figure 2 shows a chart which was produced to capture the HRA's new managing philosophy. Good fundamental management, by both central office and local jobcentres, leads to efficient use of participants' time on welfare to prepare for a job placement. This investment results in greater success in the labour market, which in turn reduces the need for future government supports.

A fundamental element of this new management scheme was Turner's 'act first, plan later' theology. He felt that the best way to plan was to create change, gather information, and then keep the good, discard the bad, and start the process over again. Turner explains his approach this way:

> The truth is that much of the academic research being done today has no practical value to those designing programs. If the times call for bold or even radical change, then we must move ahead forthrightly and responsibly, but perhaps without a full complement of experimental research to guide us.[15]

Predictably, critics quoted this strategy—otherwise put, 'Ready, Fire, Aim'—to argue their case that the city's reform effort was being recklessly, if not carelessly, implemented at the expense of the vulnerable poor. On the contrary, this process is among the most well-suited to public managers desiring speed and flexibility in responding to human needs. Especially given the fast pace of welfare policy changes, a research process that encourages innovation and then quickly adopts what works and rejects what doesn't takes highest priority.

In Turner's defence is one of the brightest minds of the past century, the renowned G.K. Chesterton, who remarked that if something is worth doing, it is worth doing poorly. By this, Chesterton intimated that many of life's important pursuits must be tried without the benefit of full knowledge, though our commitment to the cause insists we must try with our best effort and improve as our knowledge widens. In other words, it's easier to steer a car moving forward than one parked in the driveway. New York proved not only that beginning an innovation without a thorough understanding of its consequences is the political reality of big-city reform, but also that subsequent planning, assessment, and improvement can be its companion as well.

Essential to HRA management's ability to assess its performance along the way, however, was a performance management system that provided reliable data and reported progress towards established outcomes. Policy chief Andy Bush utilised the new data infrastructure to administer a measurement and accountability system that charted the course to achieving the 100 per cent work-engagement goal by December 1999. The new system, called JobStat (abbreviated from Job Statistics) identified 35 indicators that would mark the surest route to executing the mayor's mission.

Since the full-engagement goal was contrary to the outcomes expected from the welfare system for the previous 25 years, Bush and this team didn't select broad outcome measures (e.g. employment) but rather a set of key processes that helped local agency staff build the competencies required to ultimately make the work-based welfare system successful. The first significant product of this system was aptly named the Engagement Report, which listed the number of participants in work, work-related activities, or exemption status.

By June 1999, merely six months prior to the full-engagement deadline, these reports indicated that over 30,000 participants were not engaged in work or work activities. This total was not a static number of the same welfare adults; rather the reports illustrated that, while thousands were engaged in activity, a similar number were unengaged. As local agency directors gained an understanding of this dynamic, they were able to deploy strategies to turn it around.

This management-by-the-numbers approach was unfamiliar territory for jobcentre managers. The Guiliani administration's new data system replaced a cumbersome system that consumed more data entry time and focused on inputs rather than outputs. By utilising computer-generated data collection, local office directors were freed to actually manage cases in place of manipulating data. For example, one manager gained a realisation that the computer system was automatically scheduling activities for participants rather than his staff making such assignments based on need. The manager exclaimed: '[the computer was] scheduling blind, but now we can actually manage'.[16] This high-tech, high-touch strategy mirrored some of the more innovative business practices of the day.

To help monitor the 28 local offices' efforts towards achieving the full-engagement goal, Turner and Bush held weekly executive briefing sessions with agency leaders. Each local agency received monthly reports on their status, and two agencies per week met with top city officials to discuss their successes and obstacles in pursuit of the mayor's endgame. By deploying computer images and a plethora of charts, city officials created a serious and businesslike setting and provided objective criteria regarding agency performance and client well-being.[17]

Bush cites the interaction between agencies to be one of the secrets of the system's success. While the 28 local offices do not compete for profits, the JobStat system has inspired a healthy performance competition since their results were broadcast in charts and graphs. But more than competing with one another—since the ultimate goal is shared by each agency's good performance—agency leaders often share insights and encourage one another's progress.

JobStat also builds the management skills of centre managers by creating a forum to understand problems and combining the talents of HRA brass and agency director peers to form strategies to fix them. During JobStat sessions, high-performing agency directors were offered an opportunity to explain their success, which served as a reward for them as well as a 'teachable moment' for other agencies. Agency directors possessing poor numbers were not criticised for their low performance; rather they were judged on their understanding of the situation and whether they had a strategy to improve the condition.

Through the JobStat process and subsequent technical assistance, HRA fulfilled its goal of engaging all families on public assistance in work activities on 20 December 1999. The number of public assistance recipients has decreased by more than 597,000—a decline of 51.5 per cent—since the

City's welfare reform initiative began in March 1995, and is
now at its lowest level since January 1967 (see Figure 3).
Every week, more than 1,200 former recipients report that
they have a job, amounting to total welfare savings of $120
million per month.[18]

Figure 3
Stemming the Welfare Tide

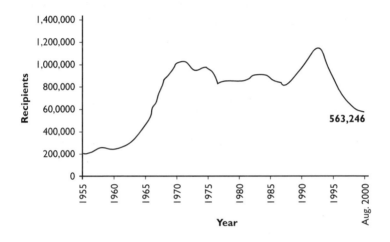

Source: NYC Human Resources Administration

While full engagement of all welfare recipients in work
activities and a subsequent reduction in welfare dependency are certainly impressive measures of success, New
York reformers sought to test their efforts against another
standard: the economic status of former welfare recipients.
To gain this information, agency staff interviewed 126
former welfare adults who closed their Temporary Assistance for Needy Family (TANF) cases in November 1997.
    The survey yielded the following results: more than half
(54 per cent) of the respondents reported leaving welfare for
full- or part-time employment; following six months off
welfare, three-fifths (58 per cent) were supporting their
family by working; and two-thirds of the respondents had
worked at some point during the half-year since leaving

welfare. Of those who worked, the median wage was $7.50 per hour and 70 per cent reported income higher than their welfare grant stipend. Less positively, only one-third of the respondents claimed to be financially or generally better off than when on welfare.[19]

These mixed results indicate the promise that is held by helping the poor escape welfare dependency, as well as the difficulty of such a journey. One former welfare recipient spoke for many with these words: 'I am glad I am off welfare, but at the same time, they [government officials] have to understand I am still poor'.[20]

No Final Victory

The challenge of making New York City's welfare reform successful in the long term will depend heavily on effectively marrying the new emphasis on personal responsibility and economic self-sufficiency with the historic protections afforded to New York's most vulnerable citizens. This struggle to blend compassion with competition (or individualism) has long characterised New York's political structure.[21] Both external and internal forces shape the tension between rights and responsibilities.

From the outside, a decreasing but ever-active minority of New York advocates expresses their opposition to reform in court battles and street protests. Two court actions in particular depict separate dimensions of the anti-welfare reform protesters' targets: the law itself as well as New York City's implementation of the law. The first prominent legal challenge was levelled at the New York (state) Reform Act of 1997 directly, which included a residency requirement for full welfare benefits that consequently denied government help to groups of lawful immigrants. This provision rang hollow in the city whose harbour includes the Statue of Liberty's welcome to the 'tired, poor and huddled masses' of immigrants who seek freedom and opportunity on America's shores.

Article XVII of the New York State constitution turned Lady Liberty's sentiment into statute via its stipulation that 'aid, care and support of the needy are public concerns and shall be provided by the state and by such of its subdivisions, and in such manner and by such means, as the legislature may from time to time determine'. This forceful language was adopted in the aftermath of the Great Depression when the City, for the first time, was unable to meet the needs of all the people.[22]

But there is a big difference between being unable and being unwilling to serve the needy, and the New York Supreme Court decided the state's refusal to cover legal immigrants was a case of the latter. The trial level of the Supreme Court ruled that the 1997 welfare law's residency requirement conflicted with Article XVII of the constitution, an action upheld by the appellate division of the New York Supreme Court. This court determination resulted in the residency requirement being eliminated before the law was even implemented.

A second case, Reynolds *vs.* Giuliani, pertained not to the law but rather the City's compliance with the law's intent. In a class action suit taken against HRA and the two state agencies responsible for health and welfare programmes, plaintiffs alleged that HRA's work-first and diversion practices prevented eligible individuals from applying for and receiving food stamps, Medicaid, and cash assistance benefits. They further claimed that this condition was a result of the City's conversion of income support centres to jobcentres, a process only partially complete at the time of the court challenge.

Data supplied by the plaintiffs demonstrated sharp declines in applicants being approved for benefits at the new jobcentres, prompting the lower court to enjoin the City from opening any new jobcentres until a matter was resolved. The court ordered HRA to create a new audit instrument to collect data regarding processing procedures. Judge William H. Pauley III of the Federal District Court in Lower Manhattan, ruled the new audits were flawed, giving little credence to the reported improvements. On 25 January 1999, the court concurred with the plaintiffs that the denial of applications was a system-wide failure resulting from HRA's hurried conversion of income support centres to jobcentres.

The Reynolds case presents interesting lessons and implications for reform activity. HRA consultant Pete Kaiser, a key architect in the development of the new jobcentres, acknowledges that the suit forced important intra-HRA deliberations that resulted in improved processes. However, the termination of transitioning income support centres (read: cheque-writing bureaucracies) to jobcentres rendered the city less equipped to prepare the poor for jobs and to forge strong relations with area employers. Anti-reform advocates for the poor who brought the case against HRA, such as the Legal Aid Society, argued that the poor are hungry people coming to the welfare offices as a last resort because they have not been able to take advantage of the recent economic revival in New York. Their position begs the question: How are the poor supposed to participate in the new prosperity without fully charged jobcentres that make work their first priority?[23]

These same advocates, while fuelling much of the court machinations, also gave rise to the street protests that aim to demonise Giuliani, Turner, *et al.* as uncompassionate enemies of the poor. Welfare Rights Organization veteran Frances Fox Piven echoes the sentiments of anti-reform forces in her criticism of the mid-90s' welfare reform direction generally and of New York's application specifically. In opposition to the 1996 federal personal responsibility act (PRWORA), Piven stated:

... when millions of women are taken off welfare, they're going to suffer and their kids are going to suffer, but so will millions of other underpaid women with whom they will compete desperately for low-wage service jobs. Wages will go down; working conditions will deteriorate.[24]

The challenges to New York's future welfare success reside not only outside of government. Whereas the advocates were attempting to thwart his initiatives via the courts and street protests, Mayor Giuliani attempted to stimulate the reform's greater impact by challenging his welfare agency with a new goal: 100,000 work placements for those who remain on the welfare rolls by the end of the year 2000. HRA Commissioner Turner acknowledged this was another 'stretch' goal, intended to underscore that private-sector employment is the endgame, and that improved services for clients are simply a means to an end. As with the first challenge, HRA not only met but exceeded the mayor's challenge.

One reason for the year 2000 success, and evidence of its commitment to continuous improvement, was the establishment of the Seaport Job Center, located on the ground floor of HRA headquarters in lower Manhattan. Seaport is a comprehensive employment and financial assistance centre accessible to walk-in applicants with emergency needs from any part of the city. Located just blocks from the City's financial district on Wall Street, Seaport functions as a testing laboratory for new programme initiatives and procedures before they are systematically implemented in all local offices.

Central to Seaport's mission is to facilitate all participants' journeys up the 'ladder of success'. This will be achieved through a four-step process culminating in self-reliance:

1. The first rung of the ladder is assisting participants to find alternatives to public assistance

2. The second rung is labour-force attachment through a structured job search

3. The third rung is a simulated workweek to develop skills and attitudes that lead to economic independence

4. The fourth rung and highest goal is private-sector employment.

Additionally, the Seaport Center is designed to help HRA officials develop, test, and implement the most effective programme approaches that can be replicated at the other city jobcentre locations. Dedicated to using the latest information technologies, Seaport has a computer on every desk to access up-to-date case information, which allows staff formerly responsible for retrieving paper files to now perform more useful duties.[25]

Conclusion

With demonstrated leadership at the top, and backroom accountability, optimism has replaced despair in New York City's welfare offices. This in itself offers promise for New York's poor that was painfully absent during the past three or more generations of welfare families. Once the nation's model for inefficiency and ineffectiveness, the city has become a national beacon in government excellence. To illustrate, consider that Oregon, long heralded as being the upper-echelon, welfare-reform innovators in the United States, has recently copied JobStat down to the same colour charts.

Mayor Rudy Giuliani has gained international renown for his crime-fighting efforts in New York, a place often described by residents and visitors alike as being in the safest condition it has enjoyed in decades. Considering this success, it is perhaps surprising that Giuliani claims welfare reform as his most important legacy. To Giuliani, welfare reform has meant restoring the work ethic to once proud people, in a once proud city. Many would have understood if Giuliani had heeded Machiavelli's caution against creating 'a new order of things' for New York's poor, though now there are many former welfare recipients who are better off because he didn't. Given New York City's success in turning back the welfare state, its steady stream of welfare-to-work innovations, and its uncompromising dedication to helping the poor reach economic self-sufficiency, theirs is a hopeful story for other big cities interested in the same.

Notes

1 Giuliani, R., 'Reaching Out to All New Yorkers by Restoring Work to the Center of Life', Republic National Bank, New York, 20 July 1998.

2 Giuliani, 'Reaching Out to All New Yorkers by Restoring Work to the Center of Life', 1998.

3 Toney, M., 'Revisiting the National Welfare Rights Organization', *ColorLines*, Fall 2000.

4 Toney, 'Revisiting the National Welfare Rights Organization', 2000.

5 Quoted in Toney, 'Revisiting the National Welfare Rights Organization', 2000.

6 Giuliani, 'Reaching Out to All New Yorkers by Restoring Work to the Center of Life', 1998.

7 Sandel, M.J., 'My RFK', *New Republic*, 6 July 1998.

8 Sandel, 'My RFK', 1998.

9 DeParle, J., 'What welfare-to-work really means', the *New York Times*, 20 December 1998, Sec. 1:50.

10 DeParle, 'What welfare-to-work really means', 1998.

11 Anderson, E., McMahan, V., Taylor, D. and Turner, J., 'Welfare reform: can the states fly solo?', *Policy Review: The Journal of American Citizenship*, November-December 1996.

12 Quoted in DeParle, 'What welfare-to-work really means', 1998.

13 Quoted in DeMaase, N., *City Lights*, December 1998, p. 23.

14 Quoted in DeMaase, *City Lights*, December 1998, p. 18.

15 Quoted in DeMaase, *City Lights*, December 1998, p. 20.

16 Quoted in DeMaase, *City Lights*, December 1998, p. 20.

17 Bush, A.S. *et al.*, 'New York's JobStat Program', HRA, July 2000.

18 Giuliani, R., Editorial, *Filipino Recorder*, 14 September 2000, p. 28.

19 Bush, A.S. *et al.*, HRA Working Paper: 'Leaving Welfare: Findings from a Survey of Former New York City Welfare Recipients', September 1998.

20 Palazzetti, A., *Buffalo News*, 5 December 1999, p. 1.

21 Liebschutz, S., *Managing Welfare Reform in Five States*, Rockefeller Institute Press, 2000, pp. 62 - 65.

22 Liebschutz, *Managing Welfare Reform in Five States*, 2000.

23 Streeter, R., 'City welfare dealt hard blow', *New York Daily News*, 2 August 2000.

24 Piven, F.F., 'Get a job: why welfare reform is an attack on all women', *The Sun*, September 1996, pp. 10-14.

25 The Seaport Center, HRA, July 2000.

Index